Vacation Re...
Ocean...
Jeannine...
JMdresch@...ionline.net
(H) 1-732-246-3292

Heavenly Weekends

Luxury 1BR
732-610-0038
Vac. rental
weekly/monthly
_____

Summer Rental
Century 21
732-974-7166
www.c21coastal.org
ask for: Jean Hones

UNIVERSE • NEW YORK

Heavenly Weekends

TRAVEL *without a* CAR

----

55 DAY TRIPS,
OVERNIGHT, *and*
WEEKEND GETAWAYS
near NEW YORK

SUSAN CLEMETT *&*
GENA VANDESTIENNE

With illustrations by Molly O'Gorman

First published in the United States of America in 2003
by UNIVERSE PUBLISHING
A Division of Rizzoli International Publications, Inc.
300 Park Avenue South
New York, NY 10010
www.rizzoliusa.com

2003 2004 2005 2006 2007/ 10 9 8 7 6 5 4 3 2 1

Printed in the United States

ISBN: 0-7893-0858-4
Second Edition

Library of Congress Catalog Control Number: 2002115759

Table of Contents

Introduction *10*

One Hour *or* Less

CONNECTICUT

Greenwich ... *mansions, millionaires,*

and the Bruce Museum *16*

Old Greenwich ... *New England charm;*

Hyatt luxury *19*

South Norwalk ... *artsy flair;*

turn-of-the-century charm *22*

NEW JERSEY

Boonton ... *intriguing old-time town often mentioned on the*

HBO series, The Sopranos *25*

Long Branch ... *full service spa; oceanfront boardwalk* *28*

Milburn ... *way off Broadway at the*

Paper Mill Playhouse *30*

New Brunswick ... *home of Rutgers University;*

world-famous art museum *32*

Princeton ... *gorgeous university town;*

lovely Palmer Square *37*

Red Bank ... *paradise for antiques lovers* *42*

Verona Park ... *paddleboats and waterside dining* *45*

Mitsuwa Marketplace, Edgewater ... *Tokyo on the Hudson* *47*

NEW YORK

Clark Gardens ... *a lush and lovely secret garden*

in Long Island *49*

Long Beach, Long Island . . . *easy ocean getaway*   *51*

Old Bethpage Village, Long Island . . .

restored colonial village   *53*

Rye . . . *old-fashioned amusement park featured*

in the movie Big   *55*

Tappan . . . *George Washington really slept here*   *58*

Van Cortlandt Manor . . . *the legacy of the Dutch*   *62*

One *and a* Half *to* Two Hours

CONNECTICUT

Cannondale Village, Wilton . . . *home on the grange*   *66*

Silvermine Tavern, New Canaan . . . *sixteenth-century*

inn nestled in the lush Connecticut countryside   *68*

NEW JERSEY

Clinton . . . *a beautiful hamlet on the South Raritan River*   *72*

Dover . . . *a Sunday flea market extravaganza*   *76*

Flemington . . . *famous factory outlets;*

Americana main street   *78*

Frenchtown . . . *enchanting village on the Delaware*   *81*

Lambertville . . . *views of riverbanks;*

birthplace of bobby pins   *83*

Mount Tabor . . . *a storybook village*   *86*

Ocean Grove . . . *the jewel of the North Jersey coast*   *88*

NEW YORK

Cold Spring . . . *charming Hudson river village with*

breathtaking views   *92*

Hudson River Cruise, New York Waterways . . . *historic*

homes in the Sleepy Hollow region   *96*

Kingston . . . *Holland meets the Wild West*   *102*

Train / Srafare?

Nyack . . . *lively old-fashioned waterfront village*   106

Piermont . . . *gussied-up 1930s town where Woody Allen*

filmed the The Purple Rose of Cairo   109

Storm King Mountain . . . *a mountaintop*

scupture museum   111

PENNSYLVANIA

Easton . . . *home of Crayola factory—*

a treat for kids of all ages   113

Kutztown . . . *a stretch of Pennsyvania becomes the scene of*

a classic country fair   116

Milford . . . *a shopping oasis in the Poconos*   118

New Hope . . . *arts, crafts, and a mule barge along*

the Delaware Canal   121

Peddler's Village . . . *shopping—colonial style,*

and a magical of merry-go-round   125

✳   **Philadelphia** . . . *Society Hill; Old City;*

Independence Park   128

Sesame Place (Langhorne) . . . *we can tell you how to get,*

how to get to Sesame Place   133

Two *and a* Half Hours
CONNECTICUT

Essex . . . *"one of the prettiest villages in America"*   140

Southbury . . . *a great resort for*

the whole family   141

NEW JERSEY

Atlantic City . . . *not for gamblers only*   146

NEW YORK

Omega Institute . . . *a sleepaway camp for adults*   149

Rhinebeck . . . *home of America's oldest inn*   *153*

Sag Harbor, Long Island . . . *charming nineteenth-century whaling village*   *156*

Woodstock . . . *echoes of the 1960s*   *160*

PENNSYLVANIA

Bethlehem . . . *repository of Moravian culture*   *163*

Three *to* Four Hours

CONNECTICUT

Mystic . . . *historic seaport with tall ships and soaring church spires*   *177*

MARYLAND

Baltimore . . . *glorious Inner Harbor; Fells Point— a delightful fishing village*   *180*

MASSACHUSETTS

Kripalu Center, Lenox . . . *health and yoga retreat in a breathtaking setting*   *184*

Lenox . . . *cultural center in the foothills of the Berkshire Mountains*   *187*

Stockbridge . . . *welcome to Norman Rockwell country*   *191*

PENNSYLVANIA

Jim Thorpe. . . *America's little Switzerland in the foothills of the Poconos*   *170*

Lancaster . . . *center of Amish life and culture*   *195*

WE ARE TWO WOMEN who live and work in Manhattan and have a passion for exploring the towns, villages, and cities surrounding New York City during the weekends. Our weekend voyages have brought a tremendous sense of joy and liberation to our lives, and have provided us with the physical and emotional resilience to return to New York and cope with its hectic pace. Traveling without a car, we have personally visited every town and stayed at every hotel, inn, and bed and breakfast we feature.

We enjoyed our adventures so much that we created this book to share our experiences with you, so that you too can take advantage of New York's proximity to such a spectacular array of amazing getaways. Whether you're a couple, good friends, a family, mother and daughter, father and son, single . . . or tourist from out of town or out of country, you'll discover a wide variety of destinations in this book beyond the boundaries of New York to delight and surprise you.

Since like many New Yorkers, neither of us owns a car, we have targeted destinations that are easily accessible by public transportation and offer lodging facilities within close proximity of the train or bus station. Furthermore, many hotels will send a courtesy van to pick up and return you to the station. Otherwise, taxis are always an option and are usually fairly economical.

Board the Train

Trains have always been a source of fascination and excitement for children—even after they become adults.

Many of our destinations, a number of them particularly suited for youngsters, can be reached by train. The train ride adds a sense of adventure to the entire trip.

Get on the Bus

One advantage we discovered of traveling by bus is that it provides the opportunity to see what life is like on the main streets of towns and villages. It is also a great way to take in the exquisite scenery of the region. And you might be pleasantly surprised to hear that most buses we traveled on were extremely comfortable—with reclining seats, overhead reading lights, and air vents. By the way, if you haven't paid a visit to the once maligned Port Authority bus station, it now has a number of pleasant eateries, a wide range of shops and vendors, and no panhandling is permitted. Soothing classical music plays on the PA system to help relax the tensest of travelers.

Off-season is in-season

We recommend off-season stays for the more popular seasonal resort areas because in-season stays require advance planning and a willingness to put up with crowds—and of course, are generally much more costly. For example, you can spend a cold winter night or two in a spacious guesthouse in the Berkshires. The temperature outside might be too chilly for the Tanglewood crowd or the foliage seekers but your woodburning fireplace and canopy bed and an open bottle of port or sherry awaiting you in the plush antique-filled lobby will certainly warm your spirits.

The extended weekend

A good way to extend your overnight stay at hotels is to arrive at your destination Saturday morning (even if your room will not be ready and check-in time is not until 2 or 4 P.M.). You can drop off your bags and begin your weekend adventures as soon as you arrive. When you check in, request a late checkout for the following day. Often this is possible and ensures you a relaxing morning that you can spend at the pool, having a leisurely brunch or just indulging in a Sunday morning sleep-in without having to pack your belongings before the maid arrives at 11 A.M. In any case, most hotels and inns are glad to hold your bags for the afternoon so you that can continue to explore the town and use the facilities until it's time to return to the city Sunday evening.

Explore

We offer restaurant recommendations for each destination and provide telephone numbers when advance reservations are necessary, as they often are. Check with your innkeeper or hotel staff about current restaurant changes such as openings and closings. But we encourage you to explore and discover your own favorites.

More information

If you'd like more information about a town you want to visit, call the Chamber of Commerce or historical society (we provide many of these telephone numbers in the text) or inquire at the hotel or inn where you plan to stay. You may also be able to track down some useful information on the World Wide Web.

Useful Transportation Numbers

TRAINS:

Amtrak	800-872-7245
	212-630-6400
Long Island Railroad	718-217-5477
Metro North	212-532-4900

BUSES:

Port Authority Bus Terminal	212-564-8484
Academy 1-800·242·1339	~~212-964-6000~~
Adirondack Trailways	800-858-8555
Bonanza	800-556-3815
DeCamp	201-783-7500
Greyhound	800-872-7245
Hampton Jitneys	800-936-0449/0440
Lakeland	973-366-0600
New Jersey Transit	201-212-8484
Omega Charter	800-944-1001
Red & Tan Lines	800-772-3689
Short Line	800-631-8405
Surburban Lines	800-222-9492
Trailways	800-343-9999
Transbridge	800-962-9135

One

Hour

or

Less

Greenwich, CT

... mansions, millionaires, and the Bruce Museum.

DAY OR WEEKEND TRIP; KID-FRIENDLY

Getting There

Metro-North trains (212-532-4900) leave Grand Central Station for Greenwich, Connecticut, throughout the day. When you get off the train, walk down the hill to the busiest street in town—Greenwich Avenue.

Being There: Then and Now

In the mid-1800s when the railroad came to town, Greenwich developed as a resort area catering to New Yorkers who lived less than an hour away by train. Gracious hotels and estates were built by Gimbel, Havemeyer, and Rockefeller along the shore of Long Island Sound.

Today it's a sophisticated suburban community with large homes, beautiful shops, and elegant restaurants. Little parks provide resting spots, and there's a small-town atmosphere that attracts shoppers from neighboring towns.

Seeing and Doing

The Bruce Museum (One Museum Drive, 203-869-0376) was once the residence of Robert Bruce, a successful textile manufacturer. In 1908, he bequeathed his Victorian stone mansion on a hill overlooking the harbor to the town, with the understanding that it would be turned into a public museum of history and art. The Bruce Museum became so popular that a large and stunning new facility opened its doors in 1933.

The Bruce Museum is a short walk from the train station. When you leave the station, turn left and walk along Steamboat Road until you come to Museum Drive, on your left. Walk up the hill to the museum. This is a perfect place to take children of all ages. The little ones will enjoy the big outdoor playground.

The Bruce boasts a sizable collection of American Impressionist art and an environmental science exhibit that includes a woodland diorama recreating early spring 500 years ago along the Sound. The Marine Room features living specimens from the Long Island Sound in a large touch tank—visitors are permitted to hold, stroke, and handle the sea creatures within.

Eating There

Greenwich Avenue, a very cosmopolitan boulevard, is crammed with bistros, cafes, and elegant restaurants featuring cuisines of many countries. Maneros (559 Steamboat Road, 203-869-0049) is a sprawling, simply furnished, and popular family steak house. L'Escale is a world-class restaurant that provides seasonal outdoor dining on the waterfront of the Delamar Greenwich Harbor Hotel at 500 Steamboat Road (203-661-9800).

Staying There

If you're interested in spending the night at a luxurious four-star hotel on the water, the Delamar (mentioned above) has a lovely ambience. Many rooms have private balconies overlooking the harbor and offshore Connecticut. To reach the Delamar, turn left as you leave the train station and walk under the railroad trestle. The hotel is on your right about a block and a half away.

Old Greenwich, Ct.

. . . New England charm; Hyatt luxury

DAY OR WEEKEND TRIP

Getting There

It's a 45-minute trip by the Metro-North train (212-532-4900) from Grand Central Station. If you're planning to spend the night at the Hyatt Regency Hotel (203-637-1234), call from the station and they'll send a van or taxi to pick you up for the three-minute ride up the hill.

Being There: Then and Now

A wonderful fall or midwinter weekend combines the luxury of the Greenwich Hyatt Regency with the quaint village of Old Greenwich. Explore the village before you go to the hotel, or relax at the Hyatt for a while and then hike down the hill into town.

The architectural style of many of the homes and storefronts of Old Greenwich is in keeping with the town's seventeenth-century beginnings. Simple whitewashed brick and clapboard buildings perch on either side of Sound Beach Avenue, the tree-lined main street. Graceful wooden benches and barrels of flowering plants outside the shops encourage you to just sit awhile and enjoy this charming hamlet.

Seeing and Doing

To explore Old Greenwich from the train station, turn right and walk down the sloping road to Sound Beach Avenue. Turn right again to find the pretty shops along this main street. Turn left and walk toward the First Congregational Church, established in 1665, and the adjoining hilly cemetery with tombstones dating back to the seventeenth century. Across from the church is the picturesque village park, an oasis of tiny stone bridges, meandering streams, wide expanses of lawn, and a glistening lake. Binney, of Binney and Smith, makers of Crayola crayons, donated this park to the village in 1928.

Across the road from the park is the Parrot Memorial Library, built in 1931. The building is reminiscent of the Jefferson Memorial in Washington, D.C. Inside, clusters of wingback chairs provide a homey setting to relax.

Eating There

The Hyatt has two restaurants: Winfields Atrium Cafe, where you can dine on fine or casual fare in the gardenlike atmosphere, or you can enjoy tea or cocktails and a light menu at the Gazebo Lounge beneath the skylit lobby atrium.

A walk down the road to the tiny town of Old Greenwich brings you to a pizza place and Beyond Bread, where you can enjoy fresh muffins and drink coffee while inhaling the heady aroma of baking bread. There is also a small health food restaurant across from the pizzeria.

Staying There

The Hyatt Regency in Greenwich is one of the most luxurious hotels we visited. This striking red brick building was once the headquarters of the Condé Nast publishing company. Take a look at the historic landmark tower. Upon entering the lobby, you come across goldfish-filled streams linked by tiny arched bridges, an outdoor cafe with umbrella-topped tables under a canopy of shade trees, and a country gazebo that provides the setting for evening cocktails. The sun's rays pour through the skylight, gleaming off the crystal glasses. Shiny brass railings circle the terraces of the guest rooms that rise above the "stage set" below.

If you decide to make this an overnight stay and check in at the Hyatt before exploring town, you can unwind by the skylit indoor pool, lie back in the Jacuzzi, work out in the fully equipped health club, or relax in your comfortable room decorated in the English Manor tradition. Later in the evening, enjoy piano music and jazz quartets as you sip a cocktail in the Gazebo Lounge.

This short trip will renew you for many weeks to come.

South Norwalk, CT

. . . artsy flair; turn-of-the-century charm

DAY TRIP; KID-FRIENDLY

Getting There

Take a Metro-North train (212-532-4900) at Grand Central Station to the South Norwalk station. Walk down the hill from the station until you reach South Main Street, then turn left. South Main is the beginning of the refurbished downtown area and runs right into Washington Street.

Being There: Then and Now

South Norwalk, or SoNo as it is now called, is a pretty water-side village with plenty of artistic flair. Washington Street, the village's main street, stretches to the banks of Long Island Sound. It has become an enclave of art galleries, interesting shops, and fine restaurants with turn-of-the-century charm.

   The town of Norwalk was established in 1640 when its 16,000 acres were bought from an Indian tribe. In the 1920s, this coastal town on the Long Island Sound became a summer resort for wealthy New Yorkers who traveled to its shores on elegant yachts. The town later fell into a state of neglect and South Norwalk's streets were lined with dilapidated factories. In the 1970s, a group of artists who appreciated the unusual iron-front buildings on South Main and Washington Streets began to restore them. The buildings are now on the National Register of Historic Places.

Seeing and Doing

Meandering through SoNo is a lovely way to spend a day. The best browsing areas in this picture-book town are on South Main and Washington Streets. We chatted with a resident on South Main, who told us he chose to live in South Norwalk because it reminds him of the English village where he spent his childhood.

Children love SoNo's wonderful Maritime Center (203-852-0700), which has an aquarium at the water's edge, around the corner from Washington Street at 10 North Water Street. The aquarium has exceptional exhibits of sea animals, where you can touch living specimens, and features ten-foot-long live sharks (not for touching!) and three daily seal feedings. The Maritime Center holds a winter creature cruise and a holiday hands-on crafts activities celebration dealing with all things related to the sea. The biggest surprise at the center may be the multi-story screen in the IMAX theater, where dramatic documentaries are shown.

SoNo sponsors a number of seasonal celebrations. Every September an Oyster Festival, with tall ships as the backdrop, comes to town. Crafts, food, and, of course, oysters prepared in a number of ways, make this a delicious experience. SoNo also has a river rowing club that offers coached rowing lessons for anyone over 15 years old, on weekends from April through September. For information about schedules, call Yankee Heritage Tourism (203-854-7825).

Eating There

As you turn the corner from South Main Street into Washington Street, you notice the exuberant Southwestern colors of the Rattlesnake Grill, its window filled with cactus plants in the background and a large lizard-like creature that curves along the glass. Featured are such Southwestern specialties as tortillas, quesadillas, burritos, and margaritas.

At the foot of Washington Street, just before you reach the water, is Donovan's, a landmark tavern that's been serving South Norwalkers since 1889. Photos of prizefighters from past decades hang above patrons either seated at round wooden tables or in booths set with blue-and-white gingham tablecloths. This cozy place is great for a juicy burger and a mug of beer. The Brewhouse (on Marshall and North Main) gives you the opportunity to watch the beer-brewing process and then taste a few samples before you dine on wonderful food.

Currently, there is no lodging within walking distance, but since the SoNo area is developing rapidly, call Fairfield County Tourist Information at 800-866-7925 for information about places to stay the night.

Meanwhile, if you want to take advantage of all SoNo has to offer, you can make several day trips; it's only an hour away.

Boonton, N.J.

...intriguing old-time town often mentioned on the
HBO series, **The Sopranos**

DAY TRIP

Getting There

Take the Lakeland bus from Port Authority and ask the driver to let you off at the Boonton post office, which puts you
right in the center of town.

Being There; Then and Now

Boonton has a long and proud history that begins in 1749.
This is when the Rockaway River was harnessed to provide
power for an iron forge eventually called the Boone Town
Iron Works. During the Revolutionary War, our Continental
army was supplied with a myriad of objects forged from the
plant, including cups, kettles, and horseshoes. The Morris
Canal, built in Boonton, carried coal from Pennsylvania to
New York and also hid runaway slaves in boats, which eventually allowed them to live a life of freedom in Canada.

   Today, Boonton is recognized by the New Jersey Historic Commission as a stop on the Underground Railroad.

   The name Boonton, most likely derived from the Boone
Town Iron Works, always reminds us of an old western town
with wooden walkways and horses lined up at watering
troughs. Of course, Boontown is a northeast hamlet built on

industry, except for its one tiny wooden walkway, where the bus will pick you up on your way home. The "boardwalk" overlooks a pristine and beautiful African-American country church set in the desecrated fields where iron ore was mined.

The hilly main street is peppered with antique and collectable shops, as well as a tattoo parlor, a holistic health and yoga center, a bar that still sells beer for 50 cents a glass, and an assortment of the usual shops and stores found in the center of any small town in America.

But this unique village has a lot more going on. If you follow Main Street, on your left past the post office to Lathrope Avenue, you come to the Jersey Fireman's Homeland Museum. This former estate has provided care for volunteer and professional firefighters for the last century. The museum features a collection of fanciful horsecarts, old time helmets and uniforms and, most important for youngsters, shiny red fire engines. Admission is free and hours are from 8 A.M. to 4 P.M. daily.

Now, back on Main Street, stop in at the Boonton Historical Society and Museum at 210 Main Street, housed in a beautiful red brick Victorian building across from the post office. Here you can find brochures and maps of Boonton over the years and view photographs of "the way Boonton was." Ask about the town tour given on Saturday mornings at the "boardwalk."

For touring on your own, walk along Main Street to Cornelia Street. At the top of Cornelia Street, you'll find the Garrett Richard House and its neighbor, the Myers House, remarkable examples of the few remaining octagonal dwellings in New Jersey. At Cedar and Cornelia Streets, you'll come upon St. John's Episcopal Church, designed by Richard Upjohn, architect of New York's Trinity Church. Its combination of simplicity, a soaring open bell tower, pointed windows, and steep gables is breathtaking. The congregation held its open service here on July 8, 1863, five days after the Battle of Gettysburg.

As you saunter up and down Boonton's steep sidewalks, you notice low stone walks of a slightly purple hue—these are called pudding stone walls, and are unique to Boonton, having been shipped only to Boonton from a village in England.

A real treat awaits you at the other end of town at Gracelord Park. Meandering along Main Street, you encounter more examples of pudding stone walls, which finally lead to a stunning waterfall on the bank of the Rockaway River—you can walk along the river path, rest at the lovely gazebo, or hike the steep wooded areas to its top. You'd be right if you guessed this lovely setting was designed by the prolific Frederick L. Olmsted of Central Park fame and his co-designer Calvert Vaux.

Eating There

There are the usual varieties of eateries along Main Street: pizza parlors, Chinese restaurants, and our favorite, Heavenly Temptations at 712 Main Street (must have gotten the name from us). This gift sandwich shop is a peaceful retreat that serves delicious casual food, wonderful coffee and teas, and sells a potpourri of delightful treasures.

Staying There

At this time, there are no sleeping accommodations in Boonton.

Note: a little-known fact about Boonton is its "Janet Club." Longtime Boonton resident Janet Bennett writes a weekly newsletter called "Nosey Parker." All the Janets who belong meet every three months on a regular basis for a weekend brunch. Guess who's an official member—but as far as we know has not attended the brunches? Former Attorney General Janet Reno. So if any of our Janet readers want to join, visit or call the Boonton Historical Society at 973-402-8840 and ask for Janet Bennett's home number.

Long Branch, NJ

...Ocean Place Resort, full-service spa, and oceanfront boardwalk...

WEEKEND TRIP

Getting there

Both New Jersey Transit trains and Academy buses stop in Long Branch. If you call the hotel (800-411-7321) and let them know when you expect to arrive, they will pick you up at either of these stops. But there is an even more exciting way to visit this resort. You can leave on the SeaStreak Ferry (1-800-BOATRIDE), which runs from lower Manhattan to Atlantic Highlands. If you notify them in advance, the hotel van will meet you at the Highlands dock (for a fee) and then it's just a short ten-minute journey to your destination.

Being There; Now and Then

Ocean Plaza Resort is a place of wonder and lots of water. It splashes from the handsome fountains in the elegant lobby, crashes against the shores of the pristine beaches, sparkles in the outdoor and indoor heated swimming pools, and bubbles in the terrace Jacuzzis. There is water, water everywhere and lots of spots to have a long cool drink or a foamy hot one. Cafe tables and chairs overlook a modern brick paved "boardwalk" that bustles with joggers, bicyclists, and folks just enjoying the breeze and the view. A straw "hut" enclosure selling tall drinks and "noshes" to swimmers and sunbathers gives this beach a Caribbean flavor.

Each room has an individual terrace looking out over the ocean or the striking coastline. Cooling breezes and ocean sounds soothe you into a peaceful sleep. The hotel requests that you close the screen door just in case a friendly sea gull tries to pay you a visit.

The Spa

If you want pampering, the spa at Ocean Place is "delovely" (and delightful). Choose from full day to overnight packages that include full-body massages, reflexology, herbal wraps, hydromassage with mud or seaweed, deep cleansing facials, men's energizing facials, and invigorating walks along the ocean.

Eating There

As of this writing, the only accessible eateries are in the hotel itself. You can find light, casual fare in the pub (dark wood furnishings, cozy and calm), where we had a delicious lobster salad sandwich, or dine on more elegant seafood and continental cuisine in the main dining room where breakfast, lunch, and dinner are served at moderate prices. Room service meals are always available.

Within the next two years a "magic city" is expected to occupy the premises directly adjoining the Ocean Place Resort. Ask the hotel manager to see a model of this "city by the sea," which will feature elegant shops and a multitude of restaurants. It's currently under construction and reminds us of the seaside town of Brighton, England.

Milburn, NJ

. . . way off Broadway at the Paper Mill Playhouse

DAY TRIP

Getting There

New Jersey Transit provides direct train service to Milburn from Penn Station (201-762-5100). Step off the train at Lackawanna Place and walk until you see a huge diner. Cross the street and turn left to Milburn Avenue. To get to the Paper Mill Playhouse, take a short walk up Main Street from the park to the third street light and turn right onto Brookside Drive. The playhouse is in the middle of the block. Or, the Lakeland bus from the Port Authority (212-564-8484) takes you right to the corner of Brookside Drive in Milburn, where you turn right to get to the playhouse.

Being There: Then and Now

Milburn is a busy little suburban town with upscale shops and eateries of all kinds. Along Main Street is a lovely rose garden that leads to a peaceful park. Amble along its winding footpath past meandering streams, a lake, little bridges, and families of floating ducks. Inviting picnic tables are scattered about. But the real raison d'être for this little trip is Milburn's famous Paper Mill Playhouse.

Seeing and Doing

Housed in a cluster of wooden buildings in a cobbled courtyard, The Paper Mill Playhouse is adjacent to a bubbling brook and a darling restaurant. The Playhouse presents top quality musicals and plays, featuring professional actors; ticket prices are much lower than those on Broadway. Their repertoire during the summer of 1997 included a number of Broadway musical hits. *Evita* was in performance when we visited, and it was marvelous. Thursday is matinee day. For information on programs and tickets, call 973-376-4343.

Eating There

The Carriage House Restaurant, set in a gleaming white stone building, has received many fine reviews. It serves only those who have tickets to the playhouse, and when you make a reservation for a show, you can get information about dining there.

The train station is well within walking distance of the playhouse, but if you are attending an evening performance, have the theater call a taxi to take you to the station after the show. There are no city lights to brighten your path once darkness descends on Milburn.

New Brunswick, N.J.

. . . home of Rutgers University; world-famous art museum

DAY OR WEEKEND TRIP

Getting There

Suburban Transit buses (800-222-9492) leave from Port Authority every half-hour and stop at Neilson and Albany Streets in the heart of town, just across the road from the sprawling green lawns of the Hyatt Regency, an ideal spot to spend the night. New Jersey Transit trains (201-762-5100) leave frequently from Penn Station and arrive at the newly renovated Victorian railroad station, also in the town center. The trip from Manhattan, by train or bus, takes about 45 minutes.

Being There: Then and Now

Established in 1680, the town lays claim to the New Brunswick Center, a prominent art district of performers, craftspeople, and fine artists. The Center houses the New Jersey State Theater, the American Repertory Ballet, Crossroads Theater Company, and the George Street Playhouse.

Seeing and Doing

As you leave the bus, or walk down Albany Street from the train station, toward the Hyatt, you pass Kilmer Square, home to an intriguing mix of shops, restaurants, and services. Our favorite is Hollywood and Vine, featuring hand-crafted artifacts, gurgling fountains, and Mexican lanterns and mirrors.

Kilmer Square is named for author, poet, and native son, Joyce Kilmer who was born here in 1886. He attended Rutgers University and was killed in action during World War I at the age of 32. The house in which Kilmer grew up is now a museum—tours are held on weekdays (call 908-745-5117 for more information).

A few blocks away, on the campus of Rutgers University, is the Zimmerli Museum, whose permanent exhibits include the largest collection of nonconformist Soviet art outside the Soviet Republics. To get to the Zimmerli, walk up Albany Street till you reach George Street, then turn right and walk alongside the university until you reach the museum at the corner of George and Hamilton Streets. In addition to its permanent collections, the museum offers an ever-changing series of exhibitions, a small cafe, and a charming gift shop.

The New Brunswick Cultural Center, an enclave of theaters and galleries, is at the intersection of Grove and Hamilton Streets. The State Theater (723-246-7469) offers performances nightly throughout the year. The Manhattan Transfer, Bill Cosby, and the National Russian Orchestra all performed there recently. The theater also features performances of the American Repertory Ballet several times a year. Prices are much lower than in Manhattan. For a brochure, call 732-246-7469. The Crossroads Theatre (732-246-7469), at 7 Livingston Avenue, a continuation of Grove Street, is America's preeminent African-American theater and presented the world premiere of *The Darker Face of the Earth*, by Poet Laureate Rita Dove. The George Street Playhouse (732-246-7717) has featured performances of *The Sunshine Boys*, *To Kill a Mockingbird*, and Tom Ziegler's *Grace and Glorie*.

Directly across from the State Theater is New Jersey Designer Craftsmen, at 10 Livingston Avenue, where handmade New Jersey contemporary, traditional, and folk crafts are sold. Nearby on quaint George Street are several antiques shops and the wonderful Pyramid Bookstore, where current paperbacks sell for half price.

If you are visiting New Brunswick during the week and are interested in biblical history, walk back to Rutgers and over to 17 Seminary Place, where the original library of the New Brunswick Theological Seminary—the oldest seminary in the country—is located. Inside its hallowed halls is a collection of Bibles from all over the world. A Romanesque-styled room with clerestory windows is devoted to books of art. The seminary is open to the public only on weekdays. Call 908-247-5243 for hours.

Eating There

The Old Bay Restaurant, (reservations recommended—732-246-3111) just across the street from the Hyatt at 61 Church Street, is an authentic recreation of a nineteenth-century New Orleans bistro. Its specialty is highly spiced French-Creole dishes, but a variety of food is available, including prime steak, fish of the day, and award-winning beers from the South. Listen to live blues and jazz while you feast on oyster stew.

Sapporo, at 375 George Street (732-828-3888), which serves fine Japanese food—including sushi and sashimi—is described in the recent *Zagat Survey* as "still undiscovered with great sushi, good value, and lovely service." For lunch or more casual fare, try Harvest Moon Brewery, 392 George Street (732-249-MOON), which offers creative American food in a unique setting and beers and ales brewed on the premises (with names like Crazy Girl Golden and Sully Oatmeal Stout).

For a tasty lunch, try Old Man Rafferty's, at 106 Albany Street (732-846-6153) where you're encouraged to "Eat dessert first; life is short." Housed in a turn-of-the-century building with a cozy lamplit interior and decorated with newspaper photos of the early days of New Brunswick, it serves casual cuisine such as hamburgers and deli sandwiches. Its adjoining shop, Rafferty's, carries an elaborate assortment of gourmet cheeses, meats, special pâtés, salads, and pasta dishes for takeout. The wine cellar features a wide range from simple Chianti and Beaujolais to the best vintage champagnes.

Staying There

The Hyatt Hotel Regency (at Albany and Neilson, 800-233-1234) is ideally situated for walking to all of the interesting spots in town. Plump-cushioned sofas and chairs are arranged in small clusters in the hotel lobby. Chandeliers provide soft light and soothing notes of live piano fill the air. A glass elevator, framing four different views of the town skyline, lifts you to clean and comfortable guest rooms. Ask for a room with a view of the white-steepled Reformed Church, which dates back to the early 1800s, complete with its churchyard of timeworn headstones.

Princeton, N.J.

. . . gorgeous university town, lovely Palmer Square

DAY OR WEEKEND TRIP

Getting There

Take the New Jersey Transit train (201-762-5100) from Penn Station to Princeton Junction. There, board the little one-car train known as "the dinky" to Princeton Station at the edge of the Princeton campus. The entire trip takes about an hour. Walk up University Place, passed the campus until you come to Nassau Street on your right. Nassau Street leads you directly to Palmer Square, the center of town. Or take a Suburban Transit bus (800-222-0492) from Port Authority to Palmer Square, right in the center of Princeton. The bus trip takes about 15 or 20 minutes longer than the train, but if the weather is less than perfect, taking the bus saves walking to and from the train station.

Being There: Then and Now

The stately towers of Princeton University form a backdrop to this bustling little town founded by Quakers in 1696. During the Revolutionary War, the Battle of Princeton was the site of George Washington's great victory over the British.

Washington signed the peace treaty with England at Princeton, then delivered his farewell-from-the-army address from the balcony of a building that has since been restored and moved to the Princeton campus.

The university has had many notable students including Presidents James Madison, Woodrow Wilson, John F. Kennedy, F. Scott Fitzgerald, Booth Tarkington, Eugene O'Neill, Jimmy Stewart, and Brooke Shields.

The Princeton Historical Society (158 Nassau Street) sells maps to guide you through this town filled with historical homes and architectural landmarks. Just off Nassau street is Palmer Square, where a cluster of over 50 charming shops surround the historic and beautiful Nassau Inn. Witherspoon Street is another delightful road for shopping and dining. Look for the cobbled alleyways and tiny side streets that give this town its charming ambiance.

Seeing and Doing

For American history enthusiasts, there are a number of points of interest within walking distance of Palmer Square. Bainbridge House, home of the Princeton Historical Society (609-921-6748), is a 1776 Georgian brick house with changing exhibits, a library, and photo archives of Princeton's fascinating history. Princeton Theological Seminary, on Mercer Street, was established in 1812 and is the largest Presbyterian seminary in the United States. (Albert Einstein lived at 112 Mercer Street from 1935 to 1955.)

Mercer Street leads to Princeton Battlefield State Park—a short hike or taxi ride away. The 85-acre park was the site of Washington's victory over the British army in

1777, considered a critical maneuver for the victorious colonists. Morven, on Stockton Street, is an historic landmark built as a residence in the 1750s by Richard Stockton, a signer of the Declaration of Independence. This brick house served as headquarters for British General Cornwallis in 1777, and from 1953 to 1981 was the official residence of New Jersey's governors. Scheduled tours are available on Wednesday from 11 A.M. to 2 P.M. Otherwise, tours are by appointment (609-683-4495).

And last on our historic tour is the Princeton Cemetery (609-924-1369) at Witherspoon and Wiggins Streets, where you can see the headstones of Aaron Burr, Grover Cleveland, Paul Tulane, and John Witherspoon.

Wander the grounds of Princeton University's magnificent campus or, better yet, take a tour (tours leave from Maclean House to the right of the campus gate). Don't miss the university chapel, the third largest in the world, with exquisite stained-glass windows, each created by a different American artist. There are also two marvelous museums on campus. The University Art Museum (609-258-3788), at McCormack Hall, has a permanent collection of art and artifacts from around the world, including a collection of charming American folk art. This light and airy museum features wonderful traveling exhibits as well, and is open Tuesday through Sunday, but closed Mondays and holidays.

While wandering around the campus, we were lucky enough to come upon students singing *a capella* under Blair Arch. We learned that *a capella* contests had been held since Princeton's earliest days at this very spot because of its perfect acoustics.

There is great shopping in and around Palmer Square, Nassau and Witherspoon Streets. Elegant boutiques, craft shops, and fashionable clothing stores are a few of the fine stores you'll discover.

Eating There

A continental or full breakfast and hearty foods for lunch or dinner are served in the pub atmosphere of the Nassau Inn's Yankee Doodle Tap Room, which features one of Norman Rockwell's largest murals, *The Yankee Doodle*. Palmer's, also at the inn, serves classical American cuisine from 6 to 10 P.M., Tuesdays through Saturdays—jackets are recommended for men. Breakfast and lunch takeout menus are offered at Olives Gourmet Bakery and Deli, at 22 Witherspoon Street. Bountiful platters of Italian-style pastas and salads are served for lunch and dinner at moderate prices at Teresa's, just across the walkway from the Nassau Inn. Les Copains is a charming French bistro at 18 Witherspoon Street (609-683-4771). The family-run Annex Grill, 128 1/2 Nassau Street, is less than two blocks from Palmer Square, and is an inexpensive student hangout that serves pretty good Italian food.

Staying There

Nestled in the heart of Palmer Square, The Nassau Inn (609-921-7500) is a two-century-old colonial lodging house with weathered shingles and dormer windows that sits atop a gently sloping hill of cobbled paths and green lawns. The Nassau Inn's guest rooms feature period furnishings and comfy country quilts. Each guest receives a "sweet dreams" chocolate mint or cookie in the evening. The stone lobby has an immense hearth, where a fire burns in the winter. Red leather highback chairs and couches and multipaned windows enhance the tranquil setting. Even if you're not a guest, stop by to sit by the fire and sip a glass of sherry or red wine.

Princeton has lots to see and do. In order to take it all in, you may need an extended weekend. And if you decide to stay a night or two, you can enjoy an evening of theater at the McCarter Theater (609-258-5050), 91 University Place—right across the street from the railroad station—where professional drama and musical events (some even before they go to Broadway) have been performed since 1929.

Red Bank, NJ

. . . paradise for antiques lovers

DAY OR WEEKEND TRIP

Getting There

Academy Line buses (212-964-6600) leave Port Authority for
Red Bank several times a day. The trip takes about an hour.
New Jersey Transit trains (201-762-5100) leave regularly
from Penn Station. Buses and trains stop at the Red Bank
train depot. Built in 1878, this gingerbread-trimmed pink-
and-white Victorian structure is a fine example of stick-style
design with Gothic revival elements. It is listed on the State
and National Register of Historic Places.

Being There: Then and Now

If you love antiques, you'll be soul satisfied after a weekend,
or even a day, in this antiques heaven. The Red Bank
Antique Center is one of the oldest antique centers in the
country. Just a short walk from the bus and train stops, it fills
three enormous buildings that were factories during the
World Wars (the big red one was a parachute factory), and
some smaller frame buildings. Today they're divided into

individual shops, where one room after another is filled with every antique and collectible under the sun. Additional shops have sprung up in every available space nearby.

Seeing and Doing

Brimming over with a multitude of unique and wonderful pieces, the Red Bank Antique Center draws shoppers (including a number of major celebrities) from all over the country and around the world. To get to the Antique Center from the train or bus station, cross the street and walk two short blocks along Bridge Avenue (pass the Galleria, a beautifully converted factory of lovely shops and eateries where you might want to browse a while) to the traffic light. Now you're on Front Street and the Antique Center is straight ahead.

Eating There

Restaurants, snack shops, and pizzerias are intermingled with antiques stores. The Galleria's elegant House of Coffee faces onto Bridge Avenue. Up a few steps in the Galleria, overlooking Front Street, is Charlotte's, which serves standard American fare. Across from the Galleria you'll find Danny's Steak House on Bridge Street.

Staying There

We recommend the Molly Pitcher Inn (800-221-1372), a lovely place rich in history and within walking distance of the train station. Walk up the block from Front Street and the Antique Center to Merton Avenue. Turn right on Merton and then right again on St. John's Place at the traffic light.

Cross over to Riverside Avenue. Turn left and walk half a block to the Molly Pitcher. It's a 10-minute walk, or you can grab a taxi at the train station.

Built on the banks of the Nevasink River in 1928 by a group of Red Bank residents and modeled after Philadelphia's Independence Hall, the inn is a striking red brick colonial-style building with white trim. There are several restaurants as well as a pool, and you're treated to a stunning view of the river and its colorful marinas as you dine or sunbathe on the many verandas that overlook the river. When you register, be sure to ask for a room with a view.

Who, you may ask, is Molly Pitcher—the inn's namesake? During the Revolutionary War's 1778 Battle of Monmouth, the temperature was high and caused men to collapse from heat exhaustion. The women who followed the troops to battle to provide fresh water became so frightened of the cannons that they fled the battlefield. Only one woman remained and continued bringing water to the men from a nearby well. Her name was Mary Hays. The men began to yell "Molly, another pitcher!" or just "Molly Pitcher!" Mary's bravery earned her a military pension, once reserved only for men.

Verona Park, NJ

. . . paddleboats and waterside dining

DAY TRIP; KID-FRIENDLY

Getting There

Verona is only 40 minutes from Port Authority by DeCamp
Bus Lines (201-783-7500). The bus stops directly across the
street from the town park at Lakeland Drive, and the return
stop is right in front of the park. Buses run every hour.

Being There: Then and Now

It's a weekend afternoon in Verona Park, New Jersey. You
step onto a winding path, pass a rushing waterfall and a cluster of kids huddled in the thick branches of the "climbing
tree," walk past a children's playground with brightly painted swings, slides, and monkey bars, and come upon beautiful
Verona Lake. Ducks and geese glide gracefully along the sur-
face. Giggling couples and laughing families pump along in
paddleboats. A rambling restaurant at the water's edge sells
hot dogs, sandwiches, and ice cream from its outdoor deck.

Eating There

The Boathouse on the lake serves casual food by day and has an elegant dinner menu recommended by a *New York Times* food critic. Tables and chairs line the deck, and inside the atmosphere is a bit like a summer camp dining hall, with its stucco walls and beamed ceiling. During the winter, a roaring fire in the huge stone hearth warms folks who come to ice skate when the lake freezes over. Just a few strides up the street, on Bloomfield Avenue, is an IHOP (International House of Pancakes), a great treat for young-sters from Manhattan.

Seeing and Doing

Verona Park is a tiny replica of Central Park and, in fact, was designed by the son of landscape artist, Frederick Law Olm-sted, who designed both Central and Prospect Parks. This hilly, peaceful oasis spans 50 acres and has paths for jogging, skating, and just meandering. Behind the Boathouse Restau-rant, children can play on a tiny stone castle and imagine being fairy tale princes and princesses. It's also great for ten-nis players and those who wish to fish (the lake is stocked with trout). At the Boathouse Restaurant, paddleboats rent for a moderate fee.

Mitsuwa Marketplace, N.J.

EDGEWATER

. . . Tokyo on the Hudson

DAY TRIP

Getting There

Go to Gate 51, in the back of the Port Authority Bus Terminal 40th Street building. Tell the uniformed dispatcher that you want the Community Line Van to Yaohan Plaza. Community Line operates modern, air-conditioned, and comfortable minibuses that go right into the Plaza. The one-way trip costs less than $3.

The minibus passes quickly through the Lincoln Tunnel and wends its way along Boulevard East in Weehawken, New Jersey, where the views of the New York skyline are breathtaking. And 20 minutes later, you find yourself in a different world—where every sign, every book, every clothing tag—almost every item that meets your eye—is labeled and described in Japanese.

Being There: Then and Now

Yaohan Plaza is divided into a food plaza, a huge grocery store with Japanese produce, sushi bars, and food courts, and a specialty plaza that houses a variety of shops under one roof, selling books, greeting cards, housewares, boutique items for men and women, children's clothing and toys, jewelry, and a vast collection of other novelty items—all made in Japan. It's a great place to stock up on Japanese cooking ingredients. Most customers are Japanese, as are all clerks and cashiers, so you really feel as though you are shopping in a faraway land.

Eating There

The food court in the supermarket is a great place to pick up sushi and sashimi. You'll enjoy eating at the tables clustered in a glass-enclosed area overlooking the Hudson River.

For more serene surroundings, dine at the Mitsuwa Restaurant, a towering enclosure of foliage-covered stone fountains and goldfish ponds with striking window views of the Hudson and the spires of The Cathedral of St. John the Divine on the Manhattan side.

Should you begin to yearn for a dose of American shopping culture, walk just up the road to the Edgewater Shopping Plaza where you'll find many new chain stores.

Clark Gardens, NY

...a lush and lovely secret garden in Long Island

DAY TRIP

Getting There

Take the Long Island Railroad at Penn Station to Alberton. When you get off, cross over to the other side of the tracks and you will see the tall gates surrounding the gardens. Walk to your right and around the corner until you come to the entrance gate, where you pay a small fee to visit.

Being There

A white stone cottage sits in the center of this lovely flower-filled oasis, housing both the information center and a charming gift shop. Here you can find maps of the grounds, which include descriptions of the whimsical gardens and their tiny natural trails.

A small version of better known sanctuaries and retreat centers, Clark Gardens offers a sense of tranquility and privacy that you cannot find at these larger settings and you can leave its grounds after an hour or two feeling that you've spent an idyllic day.

Some gardens are designed especially for children so they can learn about a variety of flowers, herbs, and vegetables and how they grow. There are also workshops that teach youngsters about planting and cultivating the soil.

Wander down the curved paths past the sturdy trees, each labeled with its scientific and better-known name. You'll discover several walkways that lead to a pond where you can rest on beautifully crafted wooden benches or stretch out across the generously shaded lawns.

Eating There

Clark Gardens is a perfect place for picnicking and there are shady spots on the grounds, as well as at the designated picnic-area tables, where you can "do lunch." (Be sure to bring your own picnic foods, however.)

We know you'll enoy this peaceful place less than an hour from the lively bustle of New York City.

Long Beach, LI

NEW YORK
. . . easy ocean getaway

DAY TRIP; KID-FRIENDLY

Getting There

Take the Long Island Rail Road (718-217-5477) direct to Long Beach from Penn Station. There is no need to change trains. The train passes many waterways as you get closer to Long Beach, and the pretty ride makes an enjoyable part of a great beach day. When you buy your train ticket, ask to purchase your beach pass along with it.

Being There: Then and Now

Long Beach is the only beach town that you can get to directly by the Long Island Rail Road within an hour's time. Restaurants and shops line the main streets, and the station is only two short blocks from the beach. Walk down Edward Boulevard, or choose one of the less crowded streets parallel to it. The beach entrance from Edward Boulevard has a bathroom (cleaned every day) that opens onto the boardwalk. There are no changing rooms, rental chairs, or umbrellas, so bring your own light chairs with umbrellas that hook to the sides. There is no shade.

The boardwalk is wide, the sand is clean and white, and the ocean is beautiful. You may want to bring a sandwich from home as there is only snack food on the boardwalk, or pick up lunch from one of the several delis near the railroad station.

Unique to Long Beach are the wonderful 1940s stucco Hollywood-style homes along its side streets. Wander these streets, if you can stand to leave the beach, and amble by houses with a movieland glamour generally not seen in these parts.

Old Bethpage Village, LI

NEW YORK

... restored colonial village

DAY TRIP; KID-FRIENDLY

A Visit to Old Bethpage Village

A real-life fable by Susan Clemett

Once upon a time there was a little girl named Vanessa who often came to visit her grandmother, who lived in Susan's building. One fine fall day Susan asked Vanessa if she would like to go to the Pumpkin Festival at Old Bethpage Village on Long Island. Vanessa said sure, and off they went to Penn Station to take the Long Island Railroad (718-217-5477). They boarded the train to Bethpage station, where they got off and took a short cab ride to an enchanting reconstructed colonial village.

They entered Old Bethpage through a gift shop filled with reproductions of colonial artifacts. Tin lanterns, silver candlesticks, and homey quilts were among the many treasures for sale. Then, like magic, Susan and Vanessa stepped through a door and out into an eighteenth-century farming hamlet. "Wow," Vanessa said, as they ambled along a wide dirt road past a cornfield and into a tiny one-street village,

"This is like going through a time machine."

"You know," Susan said, "lots of these buildings are really very old and were brought here from other parts of Long Island. People really lived and worked in many of these houses and shops."

"Cool," said Vanessa, and she skipped past the village tavern (they would return later for a cold drink) and popped into the tiny blacksmith shop and then into the general store. Ladies and gents, dressed as they used to in those bygone days, smiled and offered to show them around.

Just then a horse and wagon pulled up. "This will take you to our church and schoolhouse," said a farmer's wife, and Susan and Vanessa climbed aboard. They visited the white clapboard church and the one-room schoolhouse at the top of the hill.

"Life was so different then," sighed Vanessa.

"That's true," said Susan. "But people are still the same and still do the same things—work hard, shop, cook, and take care of their families."

Then they climbed back on the old wagon, which rolled down the hill and through the village to a little fenced-in farm with horses and cows and lambs.

"I'm having a wonderful time," Vanessa said.

"Glad you are enjoying it," said Susan. "Ready to pick out a pumpkin?"

"Ready," said Vanessa. "Can I get one for Grandma?"

"Of course," said Susan. And they walked toward a patch of bright orange pumpkins.

For information about hours, admission prices, and special events, call 516-572-8400.

Rye, N.Y.

*. . . old-fashioned amusement park featured
in the movie* **Big**

DAY TRIP; KID-FRIENDLY

Getting There

Take the Metro-North train (212-532-4900) from Grand
Central. The trip to Rye takes about 45 minutes. When you
get off the train, you will be facing Purchase Street, the
main street in town.

Being There: Then and Now

If you think Rye looks like a New England village, it's
because it once was a New England village. It belonged to
Connecticut before it was annexed by New York State in the
late seventeenth century as part of the resolution of a bound-
ary dispute between the Dutch and the English.

An authentic colonial tavern, known as the Square
House when it was built in 1760, sits on the edge of the Village Green at the start of Purchase Street. In the late 1700s,
Dr. Ebenezer Haviland took ownership and renamed the tavern the Haviland Inn, attracting customers from George

Washington to John and Samuel Adams. All along Purchase Street are quaint old woodframe houses that have been converted to shops and cafes.

Seeing and Doing

The Square House, on Purchase Street, right near the railroad station, is headquarters for the Rye Historical Society and Museum. Free guided tours are available; call 203-976-7588 for schedules and for the booklet describing Rye's landmark buildings. A beautiful example of colonial architecture, the former tavern is a shingled, gambrel-roofed structure built around a 12-foot-wide chimney. A handsome porch runs the length of the building. You can tour the tavern room, a wonderful colonial kitchen, and the inn's bedrooms—all on one side of the chimney. The other side of the chimney holds meeting rooms, a counsel chamber, and even a grand ballroom.

Rye is also famous for Rye Playland, an old-fashioned amusement park that was featured in the movie *Big*. To get there, take the #74 bus from the railroad station. The art deco–style park features an 82-foot Dragon Coaster, one of the few wooden roller coasters left in the country. There are 44 more rides, including a separate area with rides for toddlers and preschoolers called Kiddieland. There is also a pool, a small beach, and paddleboats—and you can even play a round of miniature golf and stroll along tree-shaded lanes while munching on candy apples.

Eating There

There are a number of appealing cafes and restaurants to choose from on Purchase Street. Cafe Segale, an Italian bistro, is the first restaurant you come to when you leave the train station. It's open every day but Sunday from 11 A.M. to 11 P.M. Jun & Hoe, at 55 Purchase Street, serves generous meat, cheese, and vegetable sandwiches on oven-baked bread, homemade soups, gourmet salads, and pastas. Farther along, at the corner of Elm Street, is a Starbucks. Turn the corner and you'll discover Mezzaluna, a pizza and pasta restaurant, at 7 Elm Street, with an outdoor cafe to enjoy in warm weather. Across the street at 4 Elm is Longfords, an ice cream parlor where all the ice cream is homemade, using fresh fruits in season. In summer, you can get cantaloupe ice cream and sorbets made with every berry known to humanity. Kids' favorite, as of last summer, was the Oreo bombe; adults love crème caramel.

*   *   *

Summer memories of merry-go-round music, cotton candy, the weathered wooden boardwalk, and the sun sinking down into the waters will keep you warm for many winters to come.

Tappan, NY

...George Washington really slept here

DAY TRIP

Getting There

Coach USA Red and Tan Line buses (800-772-3689) leave from Port Authority and stop at Tappan several times a day.

Being There: Then

The historic area of Tappan transports you back to the time of the American Revolution. The buildings are made of stone, stucco, and clapboard, and except for the DeWint House a few blocks away, they are all clustered together, forming a tiny enclave of a bygone time.

The 1776 House, one of America's oldest taverns, anchors this time-honored place. Built in 1668, it was already well established when the war began to whirl around it. So the old tavern, which had been a sanctuary for more than two hundred years became a safe house for Americans during this turbulent era. On many other occasions, this modest place accommodated every general who served in the Continental army in this area of the state, including Commander-in-Chief General George Washington.

The DeWint House, the oldest surviving structure in Rockland County, is a remarkable example of Hudson Valley's Dutch Colonial architecture. But it gained fame because George W. slept there on four different occasions. His first stay was a week in August in 1780 when he was inspecting the Hudson River area; then again in September and October of the same year for the incarceration (which took place at the 1776 House) and later, the trial and hanging of the British spy, Major John Andre. Three years later while negotiating the withdrawal of the British troops from New York City, Washington, British General Sir Guy Carleton, and his key staff were headquartered at the DeWint House and while tendering his resignation in the winter of 1783, Washington needed the DeWint home again as refuge from a terrible snowstorm.

...And Now

The stone front of the 1776 House that was the former tavern has been expanded and is now an exceptionally beautiful restaurant with wide beam floors and roaring fireplaces. You can dine there every day; call 845-359-5476 to make reservations.

The DeWint House has been fully restored and is open to visitors on a daily basis.

Seeing and Doing

Exploring tiny historic Tappan can easily take an afternoon or even, if you take advantage of all you can see and do, an entire day.

Tappan has a charming white clapboard library, which, in addition to all the other days of the week, is actually open on Sundays from 2 to 5 in the afternoon. Cozy up on one of the wingback chairs arranged by the fireplace mantle or nestle down on a comfortable couch and browse through the latest magazines. Sadly, you can't use your library card here (unless, of course, you are a secret Tappan resident). As you leave the library, walk to the back entrance and sit on a bench in a sweet little park; geese often land for a dip in the pond.

Next to the library is a deep-red painted landmark building dating back to 1922 that houses a delightful antique and collectable shop called The Stable. Its shelves are crammed with many treasures from bygone days including cookie jars, salt and pepper shakers, vintage dolls, stuffed animals, and country blankets.

To reach the DeWint House (845-359-1359) turn the corner to the left of The Stable and walk a few blocks down Oak Tree Road, then turn right on Livingston Avenue. The first driveway on the right is the entrance to the DeWint.

Thanks to careful restoration, the entire house has the colonial charm that George Washington experienced during his four visits. Imagine you are accompanying him on a tour of the house and step into the South Room where he spent the night and the next day met with his officers.

Eating There

Of course, The 1776 House is our recommendation for dining: platters are set out on pewter chargers and the mainly American cuisine is delicious. Saturdays, between 11:30 A.M. and 2 P.M., an incredible brunch is served, including scottish smoked salmon (lox by any other name), all the shrimp you can peel, fresh fruit salad, seafood salad, an omelet station, two carving stations offering turkey, ham, chicken, fish, pot roast, hot pasta, mashed potatoes, home-baked muffins and breads, apple crunch cake, and coffee. For an additional $2.95, you can have unlimited champagne and mimosas.

Van Cortlandt Manor, NY

. . . the legacy of the Dutch

DAY TRIP; KID-FRIENDLY

Getting There

Take the Metro-North train (212-561-4900) from Grand Central Station to Croton-Harmon. Walk through the station parking lot, where you can get a taxi or go up the stairs to start your 15-minute walk east along Croton Point Avenue. Walk under the overpass (Route 9) until you reach Riverside Avenue. Turn right at the shopping center and follow the road, which brings you directly to the Manor. The visitors' lounge, where you pay for admission, is just past the Manor House.

Being There: Then and Now

Van Cortlandt Manor (914-631-3992) was purchased in 1680 by Stephanus Van Cortlandt, a Dutchman who arrived in New Amsterdam in 1638. Only a one-story hunting lodge when Van Cortlandt acquired it, the manor evolved over the years into a three-story home of brick and clapboard with a generous wood-planked front porch. A cobbled walkway, called "the long path," stretches past orchards and gardens. This path takes you to the Ferry House, formerly a colonial tavern that provided food and shelter for travelers who came by ferry across the Croton River or via the Old Albany Post Road. George Washington used the Ferry House as an outpost during the Revolutionary War.

Seeing and Doing

As you walk through the Ferry House, you can imagine colonial folks catching up on local gossip, eating, drinking, and resting in the front parlor, taproom, and sleeping rooms.

Stroll back to the main house during spring or summer, and costumed guides will escort you to demonstrations of blacksmithing, cooking, weaving, and sheep shearing. You can tour the eighteenth-century rooms of the manor house, where the kitchen bustles with demonstrations of baking bread in beehive ovens and cooking food with colonial utensils. It's a world away, but only an hour from Grand Central Station.

Eating There

A cafe on the manor grounds serves buffet-style. You can also purchase sandwiches and bring them out to the picnic area on the meadow.

One
and a
Half
to
Two
Hours

Cannondale Village, Wilton

CONNECTICUT

... home on the grange

DAY TRIP

Getting There

Take Metro-North (212-532-4900) to South Norwalk, and then switch trains to the Danbury line (on the same track) for the ten-minute ride to the Wilton Station.

Being There: Then and Now

In the 1850s, at the behest of Mr. Cannon, owner of the local general store, the Danbury rail tracks were built to bring trains directly into Cannondale. As farmlands vanished, the townsfolk left the area, leaving behind the sturdy old buildings in which they had lived and worked. Decades later, these were refurbished to become Cannondale Village.

Once a farming village with a post office and general store, Cannondale also had a grange, a wooden structure where farmers and their families came together to trade secrets and learn sewing, baking, and crafts. The grange in Cannondale Village exists today as a showcase for the tradition. There is a grange fair every August, and the Blessing of the Animals is held at the grange every Christmas.

The town held title to Wilton's one-room schoolhouse until the building was sold for $1 to actress June Havoc, sister of Gypsy Rose Lee. Ms. Havoc, who already owned the charming retail complex called Cannondale Village, moved the schoolhouse there and turned it into a tea room. In 1991, Tom King and his daughter, Marcia, bought it and converted it into a restaurant—the Old Schoolhouse Grill.

Seeing and Doing

Built as a rail depot in 1892, Wilton's train station is now called St. Benedict Guild and offers books and unique gifts from around the world. There is an ever-changing art exhibit in an upstairs loft, and the shop downstairs sells coffee and newspapers in the mornings (all profits go to the St. Benedict Monastery). Nearby, are more shops in a bright pumpkin-colored barn. Annabel Green sells exquisite flower arrangements, boutique clothing, and jewelry; Penny Alta features food and crafts from the British Isles; Green Willow Antiques sells a variety of collectibles, from folk art objects to more formal furniture; the Cannondale Art Gallery showcases local and regional artists; and the Well-Dressed Basket is the tiniest gift shop imaginable—it opens onto a shady lawn with a wooden picnic table out front.

Cannondale Village is a great place to treat a friend (say, on a birthday) to a Sunday brunch in warm weather, and maybe a gift certificate for one of the shops. Shop hours are from 11 A.M. to 5 P.M., Tuesday through Saturday. For more information call 203-762-8617.

Silvermine Tavern, New Canaan

. . . sixteenth-century inn in the lush
Connecticut countryside

WEEKEND TRIP

Getting There

Metro-North takes you to New Canaan. (You have to change trains at Stamford—the train to New Canaan will be waiting at the station.) If you travel light, you may want to explore New Canaan for an hour or two before you catch a taxi from the station (EverReady Transportation, 203-966-6866) for the four mile, $8 trip to the Silvermine Tavern.

Being There: Then and Now

If you do decide to wander around New Canaan, a tree-lined town of elegant shops, art galleries, beautiful antiques shops, and two exquisite churches, turn right as you leave the station, which brings you to Elm Street, where the town center begins. Walk up Park Street (which cuts right into Elm Street near the station) and climb the hill to "God's Acre," for a closer look at the town's two perfectly classic New England churches.

Once you get to Silvermine, you find yourself in a small pre-Revolutionary War town dating back to 1642. Silvermine no longer has a town center, but its mainstay is the Silvermine Tavern and the Silvermine Guild of Artists, a group of wooden buildings that house a renowned art school and several galleries. The area is famous for its gorgeous scenery, where old stone walls line country roads that wind past ponds, woods, and beautifully preserved old New England homes.

The Silvermine Tavern (203-847-4558), which looks out on the Silvermine River, is made up of a group of five clapboard and shingled buildings. The main one was once the tap room for men working the mills along the river in the mid-1800s. The old mill, located down by the waterfall, was a wood-turning and peg-making factory. The coach house is said to have been used as a still during Prohibition. The former gatehouse now serves as the main dining room. A nineteenth-century country store has been moved onto the site from where it was first built across the road. During its heyday, the country store played many roles. Originally a general store with supplies for the townspeople, it later became a church hall, then a blacksmith shop, and finally a dance hall.

In the early 1900s, the hamlet of Silvermine was home to a community of writers and artists who started the Knockers Club, which later developed into the Silvermine Guild— one of the oldest art centers in New England. When Otto Goldstein bought the tavern for his home in 1906, it became a gathering place for local artists. J. Kenneth Byard bought the complex after the repeal of Prohibition and renamed it the Silvermine Tavern. Byard's collection of antique furnishings, primitive paintings, and farm implements are on display today throughout the inn.

Seeing and Doing

The inn has a delightful gift shop, set back on a wide lawn with a table and lounge chairs. You can walk up the road to view exhibitions at the Silvermine Art Guild, open daily. At the front desk, pick up a copy of the brochure "A Short Walking Tour of Silvermine." The walk, which is about two miles, takes you down to the river, past farmhouses and along winding lanes.

Eating There

The Tavern is famous for its award-winning New England cuisine—especially its honey buns (a continental breakfast featuring these honey buns is included in the room rate), and the Sunday champagne brunch buffet is outstanding. Lunch and dinner are served in a charming dining room. In winter, a fire crackles in a hearth hung with antique pots. In spring and summer, you can also dine on a tree-shaded deck overlooking the mill pond and Silvermine River, where swans and ducks swim nearby.

If you just want a sandwich for lunch, you can walk up Silvermine Road to the Silvermine Market, which sells fresh muffins and sandwiches as well as daily newspapers. Sit at one of the small tables by the windows that look out on the Silvermine Art School just across the road.

Staying There

In the Tavern's guest rooms, country quilts cover four-poster beds and rag rugs cover the wide-plank floors. You can relax with a book in one of the wingback chairs flanking the colonial fireplace in the wood-beamed parlor. The walls are hung with primitive landscapes and portraits from the original Byard collection.

Clinton, NJ

...a beautiful hamlet on the South Raritan River

DAY TRIP

Getting There

Clinton is an hour and twenty minutes from Port Authority. Call Transbridge Buses (800-962-9135) for their current schedule. Ask the driver to let you off at Clinton.

When the ride is over, there is a twenty-minute walk into this historic village. Clinton is such a unique little town with so much to delight in that it's well worth the walk—especially in the early spring and fall.

Being there

As you leave the bus at the Clinton "Park & Ride," walk to the other side of the small bus station toward Buffet King where you take a right and then go straight ahead toward the traffic light, keeping to the side of the road. Although there are no sidewalks here, the cars are coming toward you and can see you clearly.

Keep walking up the small hill past the traffic light till you come to a Sprint building. Just across the road you'll see a beautiful hand-painted sign welcoming you to Historic Clinton. Cross over to the sign where the prettiest part of the walk begins.

You pass small wooden and stone homes, Queen Anne Victorians, and elegant white column houses. Soon you come to a large churchyard surrounded by the striking spires of the Clinton Presbyterian Church. The gray brick-and-slate path winds around the church alongside simple, narrow brightly painted houses, evoking a feeling of earlier times and finally depositing you at Center and Leigh Street, where Clinton's commercial area begins.

This is the then and now of Clinton because this village holds past and present together so beautifully. The work of the Mulligan family who was responsible for the creation of the village in the late 1700s can be seen all through the town today. And as you stroll past the library on Leigh Street toward Main Street, continued feelings of past mixing with present time seem to accompany you.

Clinton describes itself as the quintessential American small town and Main Street, with its charming shops, Victorian buildings, American flags waving from so many of the homes and storefronts, reflect the sentiment. Main Street is also breathtakingly beautiful and even has an old-fashioned five-and-ten-cent store.

Take a right turn on Main and, after exploring its bookshops, boutiques, and collectable emporiums, walk to the bright yellow wrought-iron bridge that crosses the South Raritan River. Before you step onto the bridge, look to your right where the 1836 stone grist mill, converted to the Hunterdon Museum of Art, stands on the riverbank.

This stunning structure is the backdrop for a small dramatic waterfall where clusters of trout fisherman—boots to their knees—stand with their fishing rods plunged into the swirling waters of the river. A walk across the bridge takes you to the famous and intriguing Red Mill Museum Village.

What to See and Do

The Red Mill Museum Village is a landmark constructed by the aforementioned Mulligan family. Postcards of this historic building have been seen around the world. The Mulligans owned both the buildings and the adjoining quarry. Their farm produced food for the community and farm animals and provided textiles for the clothing designed and sewed by the women of the village, who also made intricately designed baskets, while the quarry produced stones for homes and for cobblestone streets

The quarry is no longer in use but all of the above items can be viewed within these beautifully preserved structures that opened as a museum of rural American life in 1963 with more than 40,000 objects on exhibit. Rotating exhibits along with numerous special events make this "village" an appealing and stimulating place to visit.

Eating There

There are several eateries on Main Street but we heartily recommend the Clinton House at 2 Main Street on the banks of the South Raritan. During warmer months, wrought-iron cafe tables and chairs are set up for eating by the water. The restaurant interior is "country casual." Its mainly American cuisine is tasty and after you eat, you can wander through several shops that are part of this enclave.

Staying There

There are no lodging accommodations within comfortable walking distance. We consider Clinton to be a very full day trip.

To catch the bus back to Port Authority, retrace your steps across Leigh and up Center Street to the "Park & Ride."

Dover, N.J

...a Sunday flea market extravaganza

DAY TRIP

Getting There

Board a New Jersey Transit train from Penn Station and depart at the end of the line, Dover Station, or take the Lakeland bus from Port Authority. The bus will let you out at Blackwell Street. Walk straight ahead and you will bump right into the flea market.

Being There Now

On Sundays from April through December, right up until Christmas, the village of Dover is transformed by canopies of white tents and rows of color-filled booths and tables that wind their way through the heart of town past streets named Blackwell and Sussex (its sister town is Dover, England).

In the middle of Blackwell Street sits an old Newberry five-and-dime (a close relative of our dear departed Woolworths) which has been converted to a cozy, antique mart. There are several other interesting shops, as well. A giant thrift shop perches on the corner of Warren and Basset Highway across from the antique mart. Cornucopia, a charming shop selling a potpourri of miniature animals, salt and pepper shakers, vintage dinnerware, toys, books, and videos, can be found up the hill on Blackwell.

Dover boasts some beautifully restored turn-of-the century buildings—one of which stands at the corner of Blackwell and Sussex. This lofty building with its stunning brick façade and American flags waving from many of its windows has become the village showpiece. Up Blackwell and across the street is the town theatre called Beacon, where musical and dramatic plays are presented, as well as shows for children.

Eating There

Dover has a large population from the South American countries and many of its stores and restaurants reflect this community with names and dishes from their own particular regions. A restaurant we especially enjoy can be found right behind the antique mart on Sussex Street. Open the door to this festive eatery and you'll feel as if you are in Colombia. You'll want to move to the rhythm of its music before you even take your seat. Take a table on its brightly colored balcony and try a plate of hearty Colombian fare.

Ken's Steak House has been converted from the old railroad station to an elegant restaurant, serving fine American cuisine as well as a variety of Italian dishes. For lunch, eat in the "railroad car" of comfortable booths where menus are printed as part of a newspaper reporting events from Dover's past. Sophisticated rooms for wedding receptions, fine dining, and dancing are open in the evening.

The Laughing Lion, an award-winning cozy, pub-like restaurant is found on Sussex Street. As is the case in many small towns, there is often a time between 3 and 5 P.M. when lunch is over and dinner is not ready to be served. This is true at the Lion, so be sure to order lunch well before 3 o'clock.

Staying There

At this time there are no sleeping accommodations in Dover.

Flemington, NJ

...famous factory outlets; Americana main street

DAY OR WEEKEND TRIP

Getting There

Take the Transbridge bus to Flemington. Ask the driver to drop to drop you off at Liberty Village, the sprawling cluster of discount shops for which Flemington is famous. At this time there is no stop in the town of Flemington itself. The bus to return to New York picks up passengers at the same little grey building at the edge of Liberty Village off Church Street.

Seeing and Doing

There are at least 60 shops in Liberty Village, many of which are outlets for famous manufacturers, and you can busily browse or shop there for hours. If you want to explore the town of Flemington when you complete your shopping spree, you can leave your bags in the shops to pick up when you return to get the bus. (Remember our recommendation to use a bag with wheels if you're on a shopping expedition.) Walk through the main area of Liberty Village, past the Totes Shop and you'll come to Church Street where you turn right and walk to Main, take a left and you'll be walking toward the center of town.

Being There; Then and Now

If you are in the mood to do some exploring and shopping, Flemington can satisfy both desires. The village of Flemington is a perfect example of an American small town. Its streets are dappled with sunshine, which is filtered through the oaks, and maple trees that canopy the sidewalks. The Hunterdon County Courthouse, a Greek Revival building dating back to 1828, was the scene of the notorious trial in 1935 in which Bruno Hauptmann was sentenced to death for the kidnapping and murder of aviator Charles Lindbergh's son.

Flemington is a good place to soak up the pretty town atmosphere, lunch in a cafe along along Main Street, and move on to shop

Eating There

The Union Hotel, directly across from the courthouse on Main Street is a lovely place to lunch. Built in 1877, this four-story brick building with its mansard roof and gingerbread trimmed porches was a popular gathering place during the Lindbergh trial. At that time it provided lodging as well as food, but today it only serves as a restaurant.

Staying There

If you'd like to make Flemington an overnight jaunt, you can call for a reservation at the Main Street Manor at 194 Main Street (908-788-0247), less than a ten-minute walk from Liberty Village. This Victorian-style bed and breakfast, decorated with floral wallpaper and rich furnishings, has a cozy guest parlor with a wood-burning fireplace during the cold weather months. To reach it, turn left at Church and Main Streets and walk approximately one block.

Frenchtown, NJ

... a village on the Delaware

DAY TRIP

Getting There

Transbridge buses (800-962-9135) go from Port Authority directly into Frenchtown and stop at the corner of Bridge Street. Turn right and you'll be in the center of Frenchtown.

Being There; Then and Now

Housed in Frenchtown's first store (circa 1775) The Wooden Nickel at 10 Bridge Street is the first shop you come to. They specialize in original country crafts and country accessories for the home. In a traditional Victorian mansion that once was the Hunterdon House is The Studio, an elegant international shopping emporium selling treasures imported from all over the world, and a sassy new boutique has come to town all the way from Taos, New Mexico. Alchemy Creative Clothing features uniquely designed and hand-dyed clothing in this swanky setting at 17 Bridge Street.

Seeing and Doing

After ambling along Bridge Street, it's fun to walk across the bridge that leads to Pennsylvania, where a roadside stand sells fresh produce, flowers, and pumpkins in season. You can sit on a stone wall at the edge of the river and watch the water. There's also a path that runs along the canal on the Frenchtown side that makes for a lovely morning walk, or rent a bike at the bike shop at Front and Race Street for biking along the canal.

Eating There

Across the road from the Wooden Nickel is the Frenchtown Inn on Bridge Street for elegant dining. On the corner of Bridge and Race Street you can get more casual fare at the Race Street Café.

Staying There

Since the Hunterdon House is no longer a bed & breakfast, staying overnight is not an option at this time; however Frenchtown is a very full and enjoyable day trip.

Lambertville, NJ

. . . views of riverbanks; birthplace of bobby pins

DAY OR WEEKEND TRIP

Getting There

Take the Transbridge bus (800-962-9135) from Port Authority. The bus ride, which takes about two hours, carries you past rolling acres of farmland, red barns, and grazing cows. Lambertville is situated just a bridge away from the heart of lovely Bucks County, Pennsylvania.

Being There: Then and Now

A bustling industrial center in the 1800s, Lambertville once employed 3,000 factory workers in the production of wooden wagon wheels, railway cars, and boats. The first bobby pins were manufactured in a Lambertville factory. When the railroads and industry left, Lambertville remained a sleepy but charming hamlet of homes and handsome commercial buildings that now house restaurants, arts and crafts galleries, and antiques shops.

Seeing and Doing

Lambertville can be the first stop on a weekend excursion to

New Hope, Pennsylvania. While New Hope has an extraordinary variety of shops and galleries, it is often crowded with tourists. Lambertville, quieter than its Pennsylvania neighbor, is truly a place to savor as you amble its classic American small-town streets. There is a growing number of antiques and collectibles shops. Pick up a self-guided walking tour of Lambertville at one of the village shops and locate Union Street, where you'll find an old-fashioned five-and-dime store that specializes in antique toys.

If you visit on the last weekend in April, you can take part in the Shad Fest—a celebration of the shads' annual return to the upper Delaware River. This event features shad-hauling and fish-tagging demonstrations, food stands, arts and crafts booths, and more.

Lambertville is famous for its antiques and collectibles flea markets on the edge of town. It's worth the mile and a half walk or finding a ride.

Eating There

Manon (19 North Union Street, 609-392-2596) is a bistro that serves Continental menu lunches and dinners, while Anton's at the Swan Hotel (43 South Main Street, 988-397-1960) serves French cuisine. For more casual menus, try Hamilton's Grill, 8 Coryell Street, and the down-home American food at the American Grill Room on Church Street. There is also a restaurant and bar with etched-glass mirrors and oak Victorian tables at the Inn at Lambertville Station. We suggest making dinner reservations in advance. Ask your innkeeper for additional recommendations.

Staying There

There are several charming places to spend the night in Lambertville: Bridgestreet House (75 Bridge Street, 988-397-2503), at the foot of the bridge leading to New Hope, is a Victorian inn with cozy guest rooms, pretty gardens, and an outdoor Jacuzzi. The recently restored Lambertville House (32 Bridge Street, 988-397-0200) dates back to 1810 and has 25 guest rooms. Adjacent to the old town train station is the Inn at Lambertville Station (11 Bridge Street, 800-524-1091), a restored building dating back to 1867, when it served as the town's post office and train station. Its 45 rooms are furnished with Victorian antiques and the suites have gas fireplaces.

Mount Tabor, NJ

...a storybook village

Getting There

New Jersey Transit trains leave from Penn Station and stop at Mount Tabor several times a day. Call 973-762-5100 to find out the Mount Tabor schedule. Since more trains stop at the Denville Station, a short walk from Mount Tabor, you might want to take the train to Denville and walk back. If so, before you get off the train, tell the conductor you want to go to Mount Tabor and have him point you in the right direction. You'll come to a steep hill across from a shopping center. At the foot of that hill, you'll be entering the path to Mount Tabor.

If you take the train directly to the Mount Tabor station, you'll be right across the road from this path when you leave the train.

Being There: Then and Now

Mount Tabor is a much smaller version of New Jersey's Ocean Grove and is considered to be its sister town. Both were founded by the Methodist Church at the turn of the twentieth century. Mount Tabor's Methodist sanctuary, which you pass as you stroll through this beguiling hamlet is constructed in the manner of a classic country church—beautiful in its clean white simplicity.

A curved wrought-iron sign welcomes you to Mount

Tabor, an enchanting hilltop village. As you wander up the footpath, you pass picnic tables, a children's play area, and the bright blue rounded structure that houses the village post office and auditorium.

Now you are in for a wonderful surprise . . . you'll feel as if you are walking onto the pages of a children's storybook: the town square, abundant with wildflowers, graceful trees, and a gurgling fountain is encircled by whimsical Victorian cottages. For a child, it is an imaginary world come true, a perfect place to visit for a special occasion. (The train ride is part of the treat.)

A tiny library is tucked among the homes and is open till 1 P.M. on Saturday afternoons. To double-check, call 973-627-9508. Stroll along Mount Tabor's narrow winding lanes and you pass more fanciful Victorians, some embellished with angel carvings and gingerbread trim.

Mt. Tabor hosts an annual house tour in September (Call 973-586-1693) On this day you purchase tickets to see the interiors of the homes. The church opens its doors to sell lunches and fresh baked cookies, cakes, and muffins, all homemade and delectable.

A barbershop quartet serenades the crowd outside the auditorium. Ask one of the costumed volunteers to direct you to the home of a special grandfather who has constructed an elaborate miniature railroad for his lucky grandson in his backyard. The train rushes through tunnels, crosses bridges, passes towns, a zoo, and lots of little people. It's a magical sight that a child will always remember. We suggest bringing a camera.

Eating There

There is no place to eat in Mt. Tabor, but across the road (on Route 53) is a small shopping center where you can eat Mexican food at the Rattlesnake Café or cross to the right of the center and you'll find a simple Chinese restaurant.

Ocean Grove, NJ

... jewel of the North Jersey Coast

DAY OR WEEKEND TRIP

Getting There

Academy Line buses (212-964-6600) leave from Port Authority (212-564-8484) several times a day. The ride takes you right to the center of Ocean Grove on Main Avenue.

Being There: Then and Now

Listed on the New Jersey Register of Historic Places, Ocean Grove was founded as a camp meeting ground and seaside resort in the summer of 1869 by the Methodist Church. This particular square mile section of oceanfront property was selected because it was the one area of the Jersey shore where there were no mosquitoes! Once described as "God's Square Mile of Happiness," Ocean Grove is now often called "the jewel of the North Jersey coast," abounding in flower gardens and tranquil, tree-lined streets.

The houses are of many architectural styles and those along the ocean are set back at varying angles allowing unbroken ocean vistas and breezes to reach the town.

Walk through the town gates on a summer day and you

are transported to another time, surrounding by Victorian homes from pastel cottages to sprawling turreted mansions. (This seaside village has more Victorian homes than any other town in the United States) As the bus pulls to a stop on Main Avenue, take notice of the many colorful shops and outdoor cafes ringed with festive umbrellas.

Seeing and Doing

Tent City is still summer housing for more than 100 families. The tents—half canvas, half-wooden bungalows with open porches and flower gardens spilling out to a communal back-yard—are set around the Great Auditorium, originally built as the Methodist Church House in 1894. The Auditorium stands where Ocean Pathway, a broad, grassy "boulevard" that leads to the ocean, begins.

Still the heart of the community's religious programs, the auditorium has hosted many famous preachers, including Billy Sunday, Bill Graham, and Norman Vincent Peale. Seven U.S. Presidents have spoken there as well. The acousti-cally perfect amphitheater, where Woody Allen filmed *Stardust Memories*, has also featured Enrico Caruso, Pearl Bailey, Duke Ellington, and Victor Borge. More recently, Ray Charles, Judy Collins, Richie Havens, and Tom Paxton have entertained here.

It's fun just to walk along the seaside streets admiring Victorian cottages, one after the other. Strolling along Main Avenue, you pass clusters of shops and eating establishments, including an old fashioned hardware store . . . if you climb upstairs toward the back of the store, you'll discover a cozy antique shop in the attic. Next door is a bakery, famous for its fresh baked breads and delicious coffee. The Shell Shop offers lamps and frames, jewelry and mobiles made of seashells. Vintage Ocean Grove memorabilia can be found at Gingerbread's Teas & Treasures. Favorite Things specializes in vintage jewelry, lace accessories, boutique clothing, and penny candy.

Eating There

For fine dining, you can go to Captain Jacks at 68 Main Avenue and Franco's by the Sea at 19 Main Avenue, both of which are open year round. During the season (Memorial Day to Labor Day) the Secret Garden at the Manchester Inn, 25 Ocean Pathway, serves lunch and dinner in their spacious dining room and shady porch. For lighter fare, try the Savory Café at 48 Main Avenue, Nagle's Pharmacy at the corner of Main & Central Avenue for "'50s food" and delectable ice cream cones and sundaes, and the Pizza Shoppe at 60 Main for personal-sized pizzas with delicious toppings. A few doors down from the Savory Café is Randal's Deli, a deli by day and transformed by night into an elegant, candlelit restaurant: tables are covered by vibrant red cloths, glass soda cases disappear behind flowing drapes, and full course dinners are served. Remember, this is only during the season; after Labor Day, the deli remains a deli — even after dark.

Staying There

Among the town's many Victorian inns and B&Bs, we recommend the rambling, white-shingled Quaker Inn at 39 Main Avenue (732-775-7525) located across from the bus stop. It has clean, simple rooms at moderate prices. Its wide terraces, furnished with wicker rocking chairs and gliders, are perfect for watching the ocean and town activities at the same time.

We also recommend the Ocean Plaza at 18 Ocean Pathway (888-891-9442). With wrap-around porches and spectacular ocean views, this lovely Victorian-style hotel features spacious air-conditioned rooms with telephone and TV in each. Breakfast is served every morning at 10 A.M. on the second-floor terrace. It is so relaxing to lay back on a white wicker lounge and watch the town come alive against the backdrop of the ocean.

Another charming place to stay is the Manchester Inn at 25 Ocean Pathway (732-775-0616). Its walls are uniquely decorated with silhouettes of ladies and gents in Victorian garb. The rooms have an old-fashioned feel with wicker furnishings and floral designs.

Rent bikes $16 daily (+ overnight)
on Main st. Hardware store
Academy / Discount ~~fare~~ ?

Cold Spring, NY

. . . charming Hudson River village with breathtaking views

DAY OR WEEKEND TRIP

Getting There

From Grand Central Station, the Hudson-line Metro-North trains (212-532-4900) leave for Cold Spring about once every hour. The trip takes about an hour and 20 minutes. The train station is right at the end of Cold Spring's Main Street.

Being There: Then and Now

Cold Spring runs along the banks of the Hudson River. Beginning at a glorious little waterside park, picturesque Main Street is crowded with Victorian homes that climb up the hillside. Swans glide on the river against the backdrop of striking Storm King Mountain—a sight to lift the heart.

Some say that George Washington named the town after the cooling waters of a local stream. The land of which Cold Spring is a part was given to Adolph Philipse, a Dutchman, in the early 1700s, through a land grant from King William III. It was originally settled by the Wappingers, an Algonquin tribe. A hundred years later, the West Point

Foundry was constructed nearby to assemble parts for New York State's first steam engine. This set the stage for the arrival of the New York Central Railroad and began the steady influx of New York City dwellers, inventors, and entrepreneurs who came to the area to vacation and to start businesses. At the turn of the nineteenth century, immigrants poured into the area to work at the granite quarry at Breakneck Mountain, which supplied the stone for the bases of the Brooklyn Bridge and the Statue of Liberty.

Seeing and Doing

Stroll along Main Street to explore one interesting shop after another. Cobbled courtyards ringed by clapboard houses have become shops with wide front porches displaying elegant collectibles and period furniture. You can rest at the waterfront in an old-fashioned gazebo and watch the river roll by.

If you want to know more about Cold Spring's history, visit the Foundry Museum at 63 Chestnut Street, once a schoolhouse for the children of the West Point Foundry workers. It features a restoration of the original schoolroom, a nineteenth-century country kitchen, and the famous painting "The Gun Foundry," by John Ferguson Weir.

The beautifully restored nineteenth-century mansion Boscobel (845-265-3638) is about three miles away and can be reached by walking. If you're in a hiking mood, walk up Main Street to Peekskill Road and turn right. Walk past the cemetery (on the left) to route 9D until you reach the Plumbush Restaurant; walk along the dirt track (parallel to 9D) to the end; then cross 9D, and you'll see the entrance to Boscobel on the right. Or take a taxi, as we did (Cold Spring

Taxi, 265-4440). Boscobel's furnishings are fine examples of the decorative arts of the Federal period. The mansion is surrounded by gorgeous gardens, an apple orchard, and a lovely picnic area.

Eating There

We heartily recommend North Gate Restaurant, at Dockside Harbor, 1 North Street (845–265-5555). To get there, walk past the park gazebo along a stretch of waterfront lawn, turn a corner to the right, and come upon a plush lawn (we love to walk barefoot here) that reaches to the riverbank and a restaurant with huge windows and a patio for outdoor dining. Here the Hudson flows proudly past majestic cliffs and low mountains; massive freighters and small canoes glide on the sparkling water—it's a perfect spot from which to view the sunset. Below, under a broad white tent, there is a bar offering beer and burgers.

Festive umbrellas surround the old Cold Spring Train Station, which has been converted into a charming cafe for casual indoor and outdoor dining. It's a convenient stop for dinner before catching the train back to New York. Sometimes it's very crowded, so you may want to make reservations when you first arrive in town. You can also find several restaurants and delis (for a picnic lunch in the park) along Main Street.

Staying There

We enjoyed our stay at the landmark Hudson House, a country inn at 2 Main Street (845-265-9355), built in 1832 right on the banks of the river. Open year round, it features two tiers of terraces with views of the water and the Palisades on the opposite shore. The price for each quaint room includes a continental breakfast on weekends and a full breakfast on weekdays. Other bed-and-breakfasts to which we gave a look-see and found appealing were the Pig Hill Inn, 73 Main Street (845-265-9247), and One Market Street, on the corner of Main and Market Streets (845-265-3912).

Hudson River Cruise
New York Waterways

...historic homes in the Sleepy Hollow region

DAY AND WEEKEND TRIP

Getting There

The New York Waterways ferry, docked at 38th Street & 12th Avenue, will transport you up the Hudson River to the landmark mansions and a quaint farm in the Hudson Valley. There are free red, white, and blue NY Waterway buses that run along 57th Street, 50th Street, and 34th Street—you can flag one down and it will deliver you to the ferry terminal. The buses will be waiting for you when you return.

After buying the ticket for your excursion upriver, take the boat that goes to the place you are interested in visiting. Your choices include: Philipsburg Manor, a sixteenth-century Dutch farm; Kykuit, the Rockefeller estate; Sunnyside, home of Washington Irving; and Lyndhurst, an American castle.

Being There

You sit inside the boat in cool weather or out on deck on a warmer day. A well-informed guide tells you about the landmarks and neighborhoods you pass in Manhattan, the Bronx, and New Jersey. You learn about the antagonism between the early English and Dutch settlers, how words like "Yankee" and "Gotham" were coined and yes, even a few jokes you might not have heard about the "garden state."

When your ferry docks at the shores of the Hudson valley, a vintage school bus will be waiting to take you to your first stop—the visitors' center at Philipsburg Manor.

You enter an emporium replete with gifts and souvenirs that represent the Sleepy Hollow area. Our favorites were storybooks beautifully illustrated by Will Moses, grandson of Grandma Moses that grace the pages of Washington Irving's *The Headless Horseman*.

After you leave the gift emporium, it's a good idea to have lunch or a snack since no food is allowed during the estate tours.

While you wait to go to one of the other landmarks, you have an opportunity to look the Philipsburg Manor farmhouse across the narrow river. You may be so intrigued by what you see that you'll decide to cross the bridge and make the farm your visit choice for the afternoon.

Seeing and Doing
PHILIPSBURG MANOR

Swans floating on an old mill pond, delicate bridges with Old World charm, a simple white stone house with a shingled roof and shuttered windows, a weathered wooden barn, rolling meadows, winding paths, and men and women dressed in colonial costumes—this is the view of Philipsburg Manor, as seen from the veranda of an airy cafe on the grounds of this historic eighteenth-century farm. If you cross the bridge next to the cafe, you come to a huge herb and vegetable kitchen garden, adjacent to the manor house, then a fenced pasture of grazing cows. Welcoming you may be the farm rooster, who sits on a fence. Look up at the hayloft in the old barn and down at the beautiful Dutch hens called Penciled Hamburgs. Outside, the shaded meadow is crowded with sheep, goats, and more of those great-looking hens. Don't miss the demonstrations of open-hearth cooking, cheese making, spinning, and weaving. A tour of the manor house with its authentic two-hundred-year-old furnishings is also worthwhile.

KYKUIT

The coach that picks you up from the visitors' center will transport you into another world as you pass through the wrought iron gates and sweeping lawns of Kykuit.

So many surprises await you as you embark on this exploration of the grand estate, overlooking the Hudson that belongs to the Rockefeller family. Magnificent statues, sculpture, and flowering gardens are an integral part of the landscape. A short walk down the road will take you to the coach barn. This barn-like structure houses horse-drawn carriages, several with fringes-on-top. They were manufactured between 1840 and the turn-of-the-century when the horseless carriages dramatically changed the way Americans travel. These vehicles from a bygone era up through the 1970s are also on display in this intriguing museum.

And now a visit to the house which was home to four generations of Rockefellers. The style of the house is eclectic: there is a steep, French-influenced slate roof and colonial- and Greek-revival style porches that open onto formal gardens. The interior designer was the well-known Ogden Codman who, in 1897, co-authored a book with Edith

Wharton called *The Decoration of Houses*. Codman was one of the first designers to rethink home interiors, forsaking Victorian clutter for a stronger sense of unity. The stately rooms in the Rockefeller house are proud examples of this tasteful new trend.

The Rockefeller home is small in comparison to the Newport cottages of wealthy American industrialists. John D. Rockefeller did not believe in ostentation and enjoyed living in a less embellished and more tasteful environment. His son, John, Jr,. and daughter-in-law, Laura Spellman Rockefeller, were avid art collectors and passed this passion on to their son, Nelson and his wife, Happy.

In an enormous art gallery on the lower level of the Rockefeller home, works by Calder, Warhol, Robert Motherwel, George Segal, David Hayes, and Pablo Picasso fill the rooms. A special treat for Picasso enthusiasts waits around the corner in Gallery 4.

Of course, our description of the Rockefeller Estate is cursory, at best. When you visit the estate, you'll learn so much more about the enormous impact this family had had on our country in the realms of industry, philanthropy, the environment, and the arts.

LYNDHURST

Resembling a small castle, Lyndhurst Mansion is set back on verdant rolling meadows surrounded by tall shade trees. Once the home of Jay Gould, the railroad magnate, it's a fine example of Hudson River Gothic architecture from 1880. Left to his daughter, Helen Gould Shepard, the estate was the setting of her elaborate parties on the great lawn. When she died, the family bequeathed Lyndhurst to the National Trust for Historic Preservation.

SUNNYSIDE

This is the home of Washington Irving, famous for his stories "Rip Van Winkle" and the "Legend of Sleepy Hollow." Irving loved the Hudson River valley and bought this little farmhouse on the river in the 1930s. Through the years, he expanded and remodeled his house, adding architectural details such as tiny steps that run up and down the gabbled roofs, while keeping the interior décor snug and simple. He shared his home with his niece, servants, and many guests. As you tour the grounds you'll discover an icehouse, a woodshed, root cellars, tranquil gardens, and a lovely orchard.

Hudson River Weekend Getaway

It was a stormy day when we boarded the ferry for the cruise up to Philipsburg Manor and Kykuit. Curiously we noticed several passengers carrying luggage and we wondered why. We asked the guide and he told us they were spending the whole weekend in the Sleepy Hollow area at a beautiful country inn called Dolce Tarrytown House. When returning home, we called our contact at New York Waterways and were offered a weekend trip to see for ourselves.

Our country inn turned out to be two grand Hudson River estates. The white porticoed Georgian-style manor was built in 1840 and the handsome mansion built from granite, found in the hillsides, was built a few years later. Dolce Tarrytown House sits on 26 secluded acres overlooking the Hudson. Lush gardens, splendid views, a fully equipped fitness center, therapeutic massages, indoor and outdoor swimming pools, tennis courts, and volleyball courts create the perfect weekend retreat.

There are a total of 212 guestrooms and suites. All rooms have cheerful décor, Internet access, coffee machines, and hair dryers. There are two eateries in the Dolce Tarrytown: "The Winter Palace" serves American regional cuisine and The "Sleepy Hollow Pub" is a casual gathering place that opens at 4 P.M. for drinks and pub fare.

For reservations and information, call 1-800-533-3779.

Will you be able to squeeze in all the tours included in the price of the NY Waterways package? Yes you will! After visiting Philipsburg Manor and Kykuit, the coach delivers you to the inn at 4:30 Saturday afternoon. After a buffet breakfast on Sunday, you can visit Lyndhurst and Sunnyside if you are up to a short hike. At 4 P.M., a coach will pick you up and return you to the ferry.

New York Waterways has a myriad of other cruises and destinations. Several are listed below:

The Fantastic Friday Dance Cruise

The Latin Music Cruise

Baseball Cruises to Yankee and Shea Stadium

West Point and Football Games

Lower Harbor Cruise

Twilight Cruise

For more information about rates, place, and times of departure, call 1-800-533-3779

Kingston, NY

. . . Holland meets the Wild West

WEEKEND TRIP; KID-FRIENDLY

Getting There

Trailways buses (800-343-9999) go directly into Kingston from Port Authority. The ride is about two hours. To begin exploring Kingston, walk toward Friendly's across the street from the bus station and then cross North Front Street and walk past the Hoffman House Tavern (you can return later for lunch or dinner). Continue along North Front until you come to the historic district. During spring and summer, Kingston has a hop-on-hop-off trolley that carts you to all of the city's highlights.

Being There: Then and Now

Originally settled soon after Henry Hudson sailed upriver to explore, Kingston was the first capital of New York State. Its long history is reflected in many of its lovely homes and commercial buildings that date back to the 1700s. In 1653, when the city was destroyed by the Esopus Indians, Peter Stuyvesant ordered a stockade to be built to contain the prisoners and help ward off future attacks.

If you love American architecture, walk through the Stockade District, where architectural styles from the Dutch stone houses of the 1700s to Colonial, Federal, Italianate Romanesque, and Victorian right up to art deco are all represented.

The trolley will take you to the Round Out, a reconstruction of a lively part of town along the Hudson River, where the once-thriving commercial port of Kingston shipped ice cream, coal, and a host of other supplies downriver to New York City.

Seeing and Doing

When you encounter the historic district, you may experience a sudden feeling of déjà vu that takes you back to the famous shootout in *High Noon*. Restored eighteenth-century wooden and stucco buildings feature overhangs that shelter pedestrians during inclement weather. The style of architecture here is rarely (if ever) found in this part of the country.

Moseying along these colorful streets, poking in delightful galleries and shops is a great way to begin your adventure. Make your next stop the Senate House, at 312 Fair Street. Guided tours of the Stockade District begin here, and this is a good place to pick up maps and brochures. Built in 1676, The Senate House was already a century old when the first court was opened. Only the roof of this rock-solid building was damaged when the British set fire to Kingston during the Revolution. A museum adjacent to the Senate House displays many historical objects from this time.

The three-hundred-year-old Dutch Church, near the Senate House on Fair Street, is open Saturdays from 2 to 4

P.M. and displays, among other documents, a letter George Washington wrote after a visit there. The blurred and mossy headstones in the tiny church cemetery reflect how long ago this town was established.

The Stockade District is your next stop. A network of tunnels that was discovered underneath many of these homes has been identified as part of the Underground Railroad. In fact, Kingston is the birthplace of Sojourner Truth. For a guided tour, call Friends of Kingston at 845-338-5100.

The Roundout Landing and the Hudson River Maritime Center are on the other side of town, but it's easy to get there via the touring trolley that runs in spring and summer and stops at the Holiday Inn. The Roundout has been recreated with great charm. Lacy iron grillwork balconies grace the brick buildings that house antiques shops, boutiques, and restaurants.

There is a lovely small park along the edge of the Hudson. Cruises sail on weekend afternoons and at sunset. For more information call 845-255-6515 or 845-473-3860.

Eating There

We love the Hoffman House Tavern, 94 North Front Street (914-338-2626) a restoration of an original tavern dating back to the 1600s. This colonial-style stone pub has several cozy small rooms with wide wood plank floors and roaring fireplaces in each setting. The Holiday Inn has several eateries, and of course, there is Friendly's on the corner, a treat for kids who live in Manhattan, where restaurants like this are in short supply.

Staying There

We stayed at the family-friendly Holiday Inn (800-HOLI-DAY or 845-388-0400), just two blocks from the Trailways bus stop and about three blocks from the historic district. Cross the street from the Trailways station toward Friendly's restaurant, turn right, and walk up the block toward the large sign that marks the inn. The large indoor swimming pool (open until 10 P.M.) features comfortable lounge chairs and nearby (but out of hearing range), a baby pool, pinball machines, and Ping-Pong tables to keep the kids busy while parents swim or relax. The rooms are simple and clean, and the weekend packages are very affordable.

Nyack, NY

. . . lively old-fashioned waterfront village

DAY TRIP

Getting There

Take the Coach USA Red and Tan bus (800-772-3689), which leaves from the George Washington Bridge Port Authority Station at 175th Street. (The A subway will take you directly to the bridge station.) When the bus reaches Nyack, it turns a corner onto North Broadway, Nyack's main thoroughfare. Ask the driver to drop you off at Main Street, in the center of the commercial district.

Being There: Then and Now

The bus ride to the turn-of-the-century village of Nyack is glorious, with stunning homes poised high on hills along the road and steep cliffs that slope down to the Hudson River. Hundreds of boats with bright white sails glide and bob beneath the graceful Tappan Zee bridge, which connects Rockland and Westchester counties.

In Nyack, you step into a charming town chock full of antiques stores, art galleries, and eighteenth-century buildings with cafes and shops featuring avant-garde clothing, crafts, jewelry, and collectibles.

Nyack takes great pride in its abundance of showpiece Victorian homes—brightly painted, ringed with balconies, topped with turrets, and embellished with gingerbread trim. The ground floors of a number of these homes have been turned into shops. It's delightful to wander among them.

Actress Helen Hayes made Nyack her home, and native-born Edward Hopper lived and painted in this charming town.

Seeing and Doing

Nyack is a town for strolling on leafy streets and venturing into interesting shops. Pick up *The Village Guide and Walking Tour*, available in most shops, which leads you down hilly paths to a beautiful stretch of the Hudson River.

If you're in the mood for a bit of a hike, walk along North Broadway toward Hook Mountain State Park, where mansions overlook the sweeping Hudson and sheep graze in a meadow. On North Broadway is an old-fashioned deli—a good stopping point if you plan to picnic in the park. Your hike along North Broadway may also include a visit to Edward Hopper's childhood home, which has been converted into an impressive art gallery.

Nyack has several annual fairs. Call the Chamber of Commerce (845-326-7845) for dates. Note that during these special events, bus schedules and pick up spots may vary (call Coach USA Red and Tan at 800-772-3689 for more information).

Eating There

Broadway and Main Street offer a variety of restaurants, pubs, ice-cream parlors, coffee shops, cafes, and health-food restaurants. We particularly like the delicious Mexican food at Cafe Sol, on Main Street, with its tiled floors, fanciful iron grillwork, and splashing fountains, reminiscent of charming courtyards in Mexico and Spain.

Staying There

Although there are no accommodations for tourists in town, a day trip to Nyack is still a delightful adventure.

Piermont, NY

. . . gussied-up 1930s town where Woody Allen

filmed the **The Purple Rose of Cairo**

DAY TRIP

Getting There

Take the Coach USA Red and Tan bus line (800-772-3689) that leaves from the Port Authority station at the George Washington Bridge at 175th Street. The A subway line will take you to 175th Street and the GWB building. The bus leaves about once every hour.

You can take the bus directly to Piermont, or if you're in the mood for a walk (about one mile), ask the driver to let you off at Sparkhill, the town before Piermont, so that you can stroll alongside the enchanting Sparkhill Canal. When you reach the end of the canal, you pass Tallman State Park, a hilly woodland of nature trails with picnic tables, and a swimming pool, about a quarter mile from the main road. To keep walking to Piermont, cross the tiny wooden bridge that overlooks a reedy Hudson River inlet where small rowboats are docked. Once you pass the adjoining children's playground you find yourself in the village of Piermont, with its network of narrow roads meandering up the hillside.

Being There: Then and Now

Nearly unchanged since the 1930s, Piermont is the tiny town on the Hudson River that Woody Allen used as a location for his film *The Purple Rose of Cairo*. Since the film was shot, fine restaurants, shops, boutiques, and a shopping arcade have opened. Nonetheless, this hamlet has maintained its original charm, and it's a lovely place to stop off on your way to Nyack (about fifteen minutes away by bus).

Seeing and Doing

Shop for antiques and collectibles, dine, and then walk over to the Landing, on the Hudson, where dozens of sailboats float on the river. If you want to be part of the nautical action, you can rent a rowboat at 124 Paradise Avenue at Main Street.

Eating There

There are several open-air cafes in the Landing, the shopping area along the Hudson, and on Main Street itself. Our favorite is the Turning Point, an old-fashioned restaurant that serves gourmet sandwiches—in warm weather you can sit on the wooden front porch.

Staying There

There are no hotels in Piermont, but it still makes for a fine day trip.

Storm King Mountain, NY

...a mountaintop sculpture museum

DAY TRIP

Getting There

Coach USA Shortline has day trips that leave from Port Authority every morning. We suggest you visit Wednesdays, Saturdays, and Sundays. These are the days that a tram is available to take you along the mountain roads for a closer look at the splendid art pieces set amoung the rolling hills and lush valleys of this unique outdoor museum. The bus leaves for Storm King at 10 A.M. and reaches the town of Vale Gate about 11:45.

When you get off the bus, call Bob's taxi at 561-8330. If you don't have a cell phone, cross the street on your left when leaving the bus and there are phone booths at the gas station in front of D&B Mart. This also a good place to pick up a picnic lunch which can be eaten at the picnic tables before you board the tram. Except for the picnic tables, there is no eating allowed on the grounds. Sorry, no pets are allowed.

Your round-trip bus fare includes the taxi, which will drop you off at the gate to Storm King (the return bus picks up at 4:45 at this same gate) and admission.

Being There: Then and Now

Originally envisioned as a museum of Hudson Valley painters, Storm King Art Center's founder Ralph E. Ogden (one of the original founders) decided instead to create a formal sculpture garden. So inspired was he when he visited the sculptor David Smith by the grouping of pieces in the fields around Smith's home that Ogden decided to place works in pivotal sites on the mountain top of Storm King. Each work of art can be viewed from many angles, allowing the viewer to enjoy the way art has become integrated into the dramatic mountain landscape.

Celebrate the deep connection between art and nature as you discover how sunlight, wind, rain, and an exceptionally beautiful landscape impact on remarkable works of art that have found a home on 500 acres of meadows, hills, and lovely woodlands. Sunshine creates light that bounces off the works of David Smith, creating a patina of shimmer and shine. Wind twists and turns the whimsical Calder mobiles clustered alongside the historic museum building. Rain rusts and ages the huge monolithic sculptures of iron and steel planted along curving roads that climb to the top of the mountain. Nature and Art have become inseparable.

And now there are at least 100 permanent exhibits that include pieces by Henry Moore, Mark di Suvero, Andy Goldworthy—who constructed a stone wall that literally snakes through a grouping of trees and appears as a serpent when seen from above—and Roy Lichtenstein, who embellished a canoe with his marvelous graphics that pops out of a tiny stream.

Visit Storm King in mid-to late-October and you experience another of nature's gifts—the spectacular colors of autumn. For a brochure describing Storm King workshops and other activities, call (845-534-3115).

Easton, PA

. . . home of Crayola factory—

a treat for kids of all ages

DAY OR WEEKEND TRIP; KID-FRIENDLY

Getting There

The Transbridge bus (800-962-9135) at Port Authority, bound for Allentown, stops in Easton's town square at the Civil War memorial, which is surrounded by fountains and shops. The ride is about two hours long.

Being There: Then and Now

Easton was home to the Leni Lenape Indian Tribe when the first European settlers landed at Lechawitank, the Indian name for "place at the forks," the land between the Delaware and Lehigh Rivers. The town was founded in 1752 by William Penn's sons, Thomas and John Penn. On July 8, 1776, the citizens of Easton gathered in the town square for a public reading of the Declaration of Independence. Easton was one of only three cities in which the document was read aloud to the public that day.

Today Easton is home to historic museums, bright red trolleys, a mule barge along the canal, and the Binney & Smith Crayola Factory. Thousands of families from all over the country visit the crayon factory throughout the year. Here, children can watch the crayons and markers being manufactured, then try them out.

Easton has recently emerged from a severe economic depression, which spanned nearly two decades—it was rescued by the joint efforts of the municipality, the state, and the private sector, with Crayola as a principal investor. This restoration has become a model program for other American cities and towns.

Seeing and Doing

Your first stop is the Crayola Factory (610-515-8000) at 2 Rivers Landing where five million crayons are produced daily—enough to circle the globe four-and-a-half times or make one giant crayon 100 feet taller than the Statue of Liberty. On their tour, kids are encouraged to let their imaginations take flight in a special room "just for daydreaming." Visit the Crayola Hall of Fame, which displays the sweater that Fred Rogers, of "Mr. Rogers' Neighborhood," wore on his February 6, 1996 show, when he made the 100 billionth Crayola crayon at the factory. The Hall also honors Bingo, the world's only coloring dog. There is lots more to see and do during your visit to the factory. One of our favorite stops is the "Bright Idea Laboratory," where visitors can explore the science of color and light. (Some colorful history: Crayola founders, Mr. Binney and Mr. Smith, got their start painting tires black—they used to be white—and barns red.) Of course, there's a souvenir shop, and if the kids are hungry, there's a McDonalds right in the building.

A bright red hop-on-hop-off trolley waits outside the Crayola factory to carry you past a lovely riverside park, quaint old buildings, and the town's shops and restaurants.

Your tour guide describes the highlights, and the trolley can drop you at any destination along the way—the entire town can be walked in about twenty minutes.

There are several antique shops along Northampton Street, one block past the Crayola Factory. Two blocks from Northampton is Easton's prettiest street, Spring Garden Street, which is lined with gracious homes.

From Spring Garden, you can take the trolley to the Hugh Moore Historical Park and Museum and the *Josia White II* barge, which is pulled by two mules along the Lehigh Canal. The park is home to the Locktenders House Museum which displays canal boat and Erie Lackawanna railroad paraphernalia. There are picnic tables in the park if you feel like packing a lunch.

Eating There

Most of Easton's eateries are near the village square, adjacent to the Crayola factory. The Easton Sweet Shop, 251 Northampton Street, is an old-fashioned luncheonette, and Pearly Baker's Ale House, 11 Center Square, a Victorian pub, is one of the best-known restaurants in the area.

We walked across the Free Bridge to Phillipsburg, New Jersey, another village of seventeenth- and eighteenth-century structures in the process of renovation. We liked watching the hip-booted fishermen as we sat on the wooden porch of the Union Street Café.

Staying There

Just a short block from the bus stop, and right down the road from the Crayola factory is the Best Western Easton Inn at 185 South 3rd Street (800-528-1234 or 610-253-9131), which has more than two hundred clean, modern rooms.

Kutztown, PA

...a stretch of Pennsylvania land becomes the scene of a classic country fair

DAY TRIP

Getting There

Take the Carl Bieber bus from Port Authority. The bus lets you off around the corner from the fair. Before you leave the bus, ask the driver where to wait for the bus to return to Manhattan. Then just follow the signs and crowds of people walking toward the fairgrounds. Who'd ever imagine you could get to an authentic country fair by public transportation?

Being There

Quaint wooden sheds and spacious tents dazzle you with a plethora of crafts and pottery, as well as woodworking and spinning demonstrations. They are clustered near the entrance to the festive fairgrounds. Meander along and you pass shaded picnic areas, beer "halls," old-fashioned "hoedowns," (square dances) performed by folks in western gear, and farm animals vying to win blue ribbons at the 4H stalls.

There are pony rides, haystacks all around, and a huge quilt barn displaying beautifully crafted handmade quilts that are such an integral part of Pennsylvania Dutch life and culture.

Eating There

Feast on "all you can eat," sumptuous home-cooked dinners of typical Penn Dutch fare. Choose from platters of country-fried chicken, roast beef and real mashed potatoes, fresh corn on the cob . . . and don't forget the famous shoofly pie. Carry your dish to a nearby wooden picnic table and enjoy!

Staying There

Unfortunately, there are no inns or B&Bs in close proximity to the Kutztown Fair, but this two-and-a-half-hour journey is a glorious unforgettable day trip for friends, families, and children of all ages.

Milford, PA

. . . a shopping oasis in the Poconos

WEEKEND TRIP

Getting There

The Coach USA Short Line bus runs from Port Authority to Milford (800-631-8405). The trip takes about two hours. Ask the driver to let you off at Turkey Hill, a convenience store, and when you get off the bus you will find yourself on Harford Street facing the Hattree Inn.

If you're staying at the Hattree, just cross over Harford Street. If you're staying at the Dimmick (our other recommendation), turn left when you get off the bus and walk about a block till you come to the Dimmick Inn at the corner of Harford and Broad Streets.

Being There; Then and Now

Nestled in the foothills of the Pocono Mountains, Milford has a charming historic district that features interesting period buildings housing charming gift and antique shops. Many residential and business properties in Milford's historic district bear commemorative plaques identifying the provenances of America's architectural heritage. Currently, Milford offers an array of shops that specialize in country antiques, ceramics, pottery, porcelain, and unique crafts. You can also take some lovely scenic walks where you can visit a number of emporiums, art galleries, and several museums.

Seeing and Doing

Outside of just walking along the back trails and sidetrails of this village and taking in its natural beauty (which in spring and fall is quite abundant), and exploring the variety of Victorian architectural styles throughout the historic district, the next thing to nvestigate is the shops, of which there is a variety—this is when your bag on wheels may come in handy!

You'll want to visit The Gallery at 101 W. Harford Street, featuring painting and pottery created by local artists. The Country Goose, at 310 Broad Street, specializes in country furnishings and accessories. Crammed to the rafters with linens, blankets, weavings, and one-of-a-kind handmade gifts is the Hare Hollow at 322 Broad Street. The Craft Show, at 120 East Harford (12 rooms in a charming eighteenth-century house) features an eclectic collection of crafts and art piece exhibits by 200 crafters and artisans. You can spend many hours just poking around the treasure-filled grounds. The Antiques Peddler, at 157 Crocus Lane, sells eighteenth- and nineteenth-century Staffordshire and English pottery and porcelain. And Indigo Arts, at 113 Seventh Street, sells fine hand-woven rugs, furniture, and accessories created by artisans from all over the world.

Eating There

A bowl of candied sweet potato soup, fresh leeks and potatoes, spinach and shrimp soup, and wraps of your choosing are just a sample of what's available at Holly's Soup Creation, 311 West Harford Street. Holly's is open every day from 7 A.M. to 5 P.M. weekdays and until 8 P.M. weekends and its cozy atmosphere makes it a great place for lunch or breakfast.

The Milford Diner serves an abundant variety of breakfast, lunch, and dinner choices at moderate prices and is popular among Milfordites, so be prepared to wait a bit in line if you go at dinner time.

The Dimmick Inn and Steakhouse, at 101 East Harford, offers lunch and dinner in a spacious, rustic dining area featuring ribfests, steak specials, and Maryland crabcakes on their menu and a "piano man" on Thursday and Saturday evenings.

Staying There

If you like the cozy environment of a classic bed & breakfast, we recommend the Hattree Inn, at 208 West Harford Street, (570-296-2661). Innkeepers Jeanne and Al Crosby have lovingly restored this 1840s home. Each of its four guest rooms feature four poster beds, luxurious comforters, wide-planked country floors, and working fireplaces. All of the rooms include one or more of Mrs. Crosby's collection of lovely vintage hats placed on a bed poster, hung on a hat tree, set on a dresser top or perched on the head of a Victorian doll. A full-course sumptuous breakfast is served every morning. Because the Hattree is small, reservations must be made in advance.

Another place to stay in Milford is the Dimmick Inn, at 101 East Harford (570-296-4021). Located in the heart of the village within easy walking distance to fine antique stores, gift shops, and lovely streets of period architecture, the Dimmick offers simple accommodations in affordably priced single rooms and suites with air conditioning and cable TV. Having the tap room and restaurant just downstairs is especially convenient.

New Hope, PA

. . . arts, crafts, and a mule barge along the Delaware Canal

DAY OR WEEKEND TRIP; KID-FRIENDLY

Getting There

Take the Transbridge bus (800-962-9135) from Port Authority to Lambertville. From there, the center of New Hope is just a short walk over the bridge that crosses the Delaware River.

Being There: Then and Now

New Hope, Pennsylvania, is surely one of the most beautiful small towns in America. In the village, a waterfall gushes behind old stone buildings, and stunningly preserved homes from colonial times line the streets and lanes that twist through this historic hamlet. Mule-drawn barges glide along a sleepy canal, and the Delaware River flows along the village's grassy banks.

The people of New Hope played a significant role during the Revolutionary War. They aided the retreating Continental Army by taking them downriver to a neighboring town, where the army began the march on Trenton that was instrumental in defeating the British on December 26, 1776.

New Hope prospered after the war and sent flaxseed oil, lumber, whiskey, and coal up and down the Delaware.

In the early 1900s, artists who were drawn by the beauty of the Bucks County countryside established an artist's colony in New Hope that became world renowned. The interior of one old grist mill has been transformed into the famous Bucks County Playhouse. Beginning in 1977, with financial assistance from the New Hope Historical Society and the borough government, Ann Nieson researched every structure over 100 years old. In 1985, 243 New Hope properties were accepted for inclusion on the National Register of Historic Places, and New Hope is now a tourist mecca that draws huge weekend crowds. But this is a town you have to experience—throngs or not—and there are tranquil places to be found along the river, or across the bridge in Lambertville, New Jersey (see page 83).

Seeing and Doing

As you take in the sights, stop at the original Ferry Tavern, the oldest building in New Hope, at the corner of South Main and Ferry Streets. The Beaumont House (1788), with its walled courtyard, is directly across the street. In 1784, Benjamin Parry built a fieldstone house in the center of town where five generations of his family lived. In 1966, the New Hope Historical Society purchased this house and restored it as a museum of decorative arts. The Parry Mansion is open to the public on Friday through Sunday, from May through October.

Particularly worth a visit is the Ney Museum on Mechanic Street. Ney, whose art is permanently exhibited in

New York's Museum of Modern Art, left New Hope a huge body of work depicting the life of the town in the 1940s and 1950s.

When you long for a respite, walk down to the banks of the Delaware to the Delaware Canal Gardens, twenty-four riverside gardens bright with plantings and flowers. While lingering in the gardens, you can feed the geese that congregate along the water's edge at the sound of human voices. Just be prepared for a quick departure: they challenge you with honking and flapping when you run out of crumbs.

You can enjoy a cruise boat that trundles past New Hope, Lambertville, and other sites along the river, or walk a few blocks to the Mule Barge Landing on the canal for a mule-drawn boat ride.

New Hope has several live theaters, and local nightspots featuring cabaret, comedy, and music by internationally known performers. The Towpath House, located on Mechanic Street (215-862-3777), and the Bucks County Playhouse on Main St. (215-862-2041) both offer legitimate theater with Equity players.

If children are with you, take a ride on the old steam engine in the turreted train station at the top of Bridge Street. The New Hope & Ivyland Railroad, built in 1889, takes you to Lahaska and back, traveling through woodlands past several homes that were part of the Underground Railroad—a narrator points out the historical sites.

For more information about New Hope's artistic and historic highlights, call the New Hope Information Center at 215-862-5880, or drop by the Center at 1 West Mechanic Street (at the corner of Main St.).

Eating There

One of our favorite places to eat in New Hope is Canal House at 28 West Mechanic Street (215-862-2069), smack-dab on the canal, where you can dine in the garden in summer and on the enclosed deck in winter. Enjoy classic cuisine for lunch or dinner at The Landing, 22 North Main Street (215-862-5711), served in a comfortable country dining room or on a spacious patio overlooking the Delaware.

Staying There

Hacienda Inn (36 West Mechanic Street, 800-272-2078) offers cable TV, room service, and air conditioning in country-style rooms that surround a sparkling, heated outdoor pool. The Wedgwood Inn (111 West Bridge Street, 215-862-3936) provides gracious accommodations and a sumptuous breakfast in three separate houses (one is the Aaron Burr House) furnished with Early American antiques.

Peddler's Village, PA

. . . colonial-style shopping and a magical

merry-go-round

DAY OR WEEKEND TRIP; KID-FRIENDLY

Getting There

Peddler's Village is in an area of Bucks County called Lahaska. Transbridge buses (800-962-9135) leave Port Authority several times a day to make the two-hour trip (the bus' ultimate destination is Doylestown). The bus stop is right up the road from the Golden Plough Inn; ask the driver to let you off in front.

Being There: Then and Now

Imagine yourself in an English country village, say, a charming hamlet in the Lake District—where you're doing some serious American shopping. But Earl Hart Lamison was actually inspired by Carmel, California, when he opened The Golden Plough Inn and the Peddler's Village shopping complex on property that formerly housed the Hen Town chicken farm. Colonial Americana is the architectural style of these picturesque shops of brick, clapboard, and stone featuring delightful, many-paned, mullioned windows.

The Village consists of over seventy specialty shops and six restaurants, landscaped with little arched bridges, tiny waterfalls, beguiling gardens, and winding brick paths. All this charm is set in the rolling countryside of gorgeous Bucks County. Just in case you start experiencing charm overload, down the road is the Penn's Purchase outlet center, a cluster of stores selling top brand names at discount prices.

Seeing and Doing

Prepare for a shopping and eating spree. The shops sell everything from country crafts, unique boutique clothing, decorative arts, jewelry, and collectibles to all varieties of gourmet foods. There are no chain stores here.

Peddler's Village presents continuous special events and exhibits that vary with the season, many of them wonderful to share with children. For instance, the summer includes a teddy bear picnic with teddy bear floats, Dixieland music, and an old-fashioned backyard circus; September offers a scarecrow festival, and December brings a Christmas festival featuring a national gingerbread house contest. In the spring, there are Amish quilt displays, strawberry festivals, and art fairs. Children will love Giggleberry Mountain where they can zoom down an enclosed six-level, three-story slide, tunnel through 30,000 foam balls, move through mazes of net, and speed down parallel racing slides. For more information about fairs and activities, call 215-794-4000.

Eating There

Peddler's Village has about half a dozen pubs and restaurants. The Spitted Hog, housed off the lobby of the Golden

Plough, is great for a country breakfast or lunch. Jenny's Restaurant just across the road, serves scrumptious food for lunch and dinner in a colorful colonial atmosphere, enhanced by beautiful stained-glass windows.

The most popular restaurant is the Cock and Bull, a multilevel eatery that welcomes you into a charming "common room" with a great stone hearth (and colonial cooking demonstrations in winter). Also worth checking out is the Peddler's Pub, a funky tavern that features "Murder Mystery" interactive theater on Friday and Saturday evenings from September through December.

Staying There

The Golden Plough Inn is a lovely place featuring hideaway rooms scattered in surprising places all around the village (several directly above the antique carousel). Every room includes a refrigerator containing a split of complimentary champagne, juices and sodas, a basket of snacks, and a gracious letter of welcome from your host, Mr. Jamison.

Sharing with friends makes even the finest rooms very affordable. Ask for one of the luxurious suites with bubbling Jacuzzi, gas fireplace, and a four-poster bed (an additional bed comes with the room). Less expensive rooms can be found over the Cock and Bull, but expect a bit of music and chatter.

During our stay in Peddler's Village, we felt like princesses. Our room, just above the carousel, had a king-size canopy bed and a double sleighbed in the corner. Our fireplace was glowing as we toasted our host with a glass of champagne after our Murder Mystery Escapade dinner.

Philadelphia, PA

... Society Hill; Old City; Independence Park

DAY OR WEEKEND TRIP; KID-FRIENDLY

Getting There

Amtrak trains (800-872-7245) leave about every hour from Penn Station to Philadelphia's 30th Street Station. Greyhound (800-231-2222) and Peter Pan (800-343-9999) leave Port Authority several times a day for Philadelphia. A cab ride from the station takes only a few minutes to the attractions, inns, and hotels in the historic areas we describe.

Being There: Then and Now

America's fifth largest city and the nation's first capital, Philadelphia is bustling, historic, and charming—"the town that loves you back"—and it's only about two hours from New York. You can spend several days exploring, museum-hopping, antiquing, nightclubbing, and boat riding, or do a little of each on a weekend or even during a day trip. Our description here focuses on a weekend visit to Independence National Historic Park, Old City, Society Hill, and Penn's Landing.

Independence National Historic Park encompasses

most of Philadelphia's famous historic sites, including the Liberty Bell, Independence Hall, and Franklin Court—where you can see Ben Franklin's many inventions. Old City is a burgeoning artists' district adjacent to Penn's Landing where water taxis will ferry you across the river to the Camden Aquarium. Society Hill, near Independence Hall, is a beautiful historic and antiquing area.

If you have an extra day to spend, you might enjoy a guided tour to the Brandywine River Valley and an afternoon at Longwood Gardens.

Seeing and Doing

Take a taxi from the train or bus stations down to Old City, once a manufacturing section with industrial lofts and factories. Now, more than forty art galleries and showrooms are tucked into old buildings along timeworn cobblestone streets. You can walk through Old City from its border at Front Street up Chestnut Street to Sixth Street, site of Independence National Historic Park and the Liberty Bell. Walk a block to Fifth Street and park rangers will guide you to Independence Hall's Assembly Room, where the Declaration of Independence and the Constitution were signed. The visitors' center in the park provides tours and maps to all colonial and federal landmarks. For more information call 215-636-3300.

To reach Society Hill, walk across Independence Park to Walnut Street where you'll find a cluster of pristine red-brick colonial homes, some in small courtyards, lined along Philadelphia's narrow two-lane main streets. You can reminisce about the times when Thomas Jefferson and Ben Franklin strolled these very streets, and Betsy Ross designed

America's first flag. You can hire a horse-drawn carriage at Independence Historical Park at Fifth and Chestnut for a relaxing look at the historic district. A courtesy van (923-8516) can pick you up from anywhere in the city and deliver you here. On Second Street, off Walnut, is Headhouse Square, cobblestone streets surrounded by restaurants and shops, with an open-air marketplace every summer weekend in the center. Serene and lovely Pine Street, known as Antique Row, runs from the Square and sells quilts, wicker furnishings, and other Americana. Intriguing South Street, just two blocks away, with its jumble of clothing and antiques shops and cafes, is always active and fun.

Walk back down South Street to Penn's Landing on the Delaware River waterfront. You can ferry over to the Camden Aquarium (in New Jersey) from here. Penn's Landing also offers a look at a tall ship, a submarine tour, boat rides, entertainment, and festivals.

We would be remiss if we didn't mention the bright red-and-green trolley that can take you to Philadelphia's marvelous sights from the mansions of Fairmount Park (ten times the size of Central Park), along the Schuylkill River where crews row, to the Reading Terminal Market, an enormous indoor farmer's market with food stalls of cuisines from all over the world. This is a truly wonderful place to go if you have extended time.

You can also take a day tour of the Brandywine River Valley. A bus run by Brandywine Tours (610-358-5445) picks you up at your hotel and drives you through the picturesque, pastoral countryside made famous by Andrew Wyeth. The bus takes you to the Brandywine Museum, which is housed in a converted Civil War grist mill. This glass-enclosed structure has unobstructed views of winding streams, gently rolling hills, and sun-dappled meadows, a perfect backdrop for its exhibit of Wyeth paintings. The afternoon of the tour is spent at Longwood Gardens, once the home of a DuPont, now a thousand-acre wonderland of lush lawns and flower gardens. Since it's not possible to get to the Brandywine Valley in Delaware from New York City without a car, we were particularly excited to discover this tour from Philadelphia.

Eating There

One of our favorite restaurants is City Tavern on Second Street. Lace-capped waitresses serve Early American cuisine in an old, recently restored colonial inn, with wide plank floors, pine tables, and stone hearths decorated with pewter plates and mugs. We love the warm and intimate ambiance, and highly recommend it for maintaining a colonial-Philadelphia frame of mind.

Ristorante Panorama, at Penn's View Hotel (at Front and Market Streets, 215-922-7600) in Old City, is a beautiful spot that feels like a garden in Italy. The restaurant's famous wine bar offers one hundred and twenty different wines by the glass, and the bartender is quite knowledgable. We enjoyed sampling the "Panoramic Flight" which offers five different international wines served in one-ounce glasses..

In Philadelphia you must also have a cheese-steak sandwich. Stand in line at Jim's Steaks at Fourth and South Streets, and decide whether to have yours with (onions) or without.

Staying There

The Penn's View Hotel, a historic landmark at Front and Market Streets (215-922-7600), is located in Old City within a stone's throw of all the special places we love to visit. Its forty guest rooms are decorated with distinctive Old World charm. For a luxurious visit, request a room with a Jacuzzi and fireplace. A generous continental breakfast buffet is included, and weekend packages are available.

The Independence Park Inn, at 235 Chestnut Street (800-624-2988), is a lovely small hotel, adjacent to Philadelphia's historic square mile. This Best Western Hotel offers guest rooms with high ceilings, a complimentary breakfast in a glass-enclosed courtyard, and a grand lobby with a roaring fireplace.

Sesame Place, PA

...we can tell you how to get, how to get to Sesame Street...

DAY OR WEEKEND TRIP

Getting There

If you're the parent, grandparent, aunt, uncle, or friend of any small child, you can't help but be familiar with the *Sesame Street* refrain that opens the show: "can you tell me how to get, how to get to Sesame Street?" Well, we can tell you how to get to Sesame Street! You'll find it re-created at Sesame Place, a phenomenal amusement park, based on PBS's long-running children's program. So here goes:

New Jersey Transit (973-762-5100) trains leave from Penn Station several times a day and take you to Trenton, New Jersey, where you catch the Septa bus just outside the train station. The train trip to Trenton takes about an hour and 20 minutes and the bus ride to Langhorne, Pa. is about an hour. Ask at the train station for the bus schedule. If there's more than a half-hour wait, you might want to step into the Roy Rogers restaurant for a quick snack. If you'd like to get to your destination sooner, you might opt to take a taxi outside the station. The price is rather high ($25-$27 when we took it one way); but the ride to Sesame Place or to the Sheraton takes less than ten minutes.

Seeing and Doing

Sesame Place is a thrilling water park for children between the ages of two and thirteen. Of course, infants and toddlers may come along and even join in a few activities, as long as adults keep a close eye on them.

There are 14 acres of water attractions, play activities, gift shops, and restaurants. Children's shouts and laughter ring out from the various water rides, several of which are as high as two or three buildings, while others have nets to climb over, mazes to climb through, and tubes to navigate. After these adventures, it's time to stand beneath a cooling waterfall or relax on an inner tube that carries you down Big Bird's rambling river, a 1,000-foot creek that runs through the park

Now onto dry land. Your little ones won't be able to resist the Count's Ballroom, where 100,000 plastic balls are waiting for the next batch of children to scream with delight as they jump, tumble, roll, and tunnel through this colorful circular mass. Later, they can find their way through a forest of lightweight punching bags, test their sense of balance on Bert's balancing beams, slide down huge sliding boards hung below nets and ladders, and of course, take the family for a ride on the vapor roller coaster.

Your teens may want to take part in a teen party where they can disc jockey and dance to the coolest tunes. This is good time to stroll over to the life-size replica of Sesame Street, a representation of the same charming street and characters that have been captivating children for more than three decades. Here your children can speak to Big Bird, shake hands with Ernie, and hang out with the Cookie

Monster and the rest of the Sesame Street crowd. (Parents, don't expect these characters to speak back—the folks who run the place don't want the children to get upset when the voices of their favorite characters differ from those they hear on television each day.)

We have only described a fraction of the activities that go on at Sesame Place. To receive a brochure and map of everything to do and see, call 215-752-7070.

Eating There

There are plenty of places to dine on the grounds of Sesame Place. Snuffy's Snack Bar provides hot dogs and ice cream specials; Captain Ernie's Grill serves turkey sandwiches, cheeseburgers, chicken fingers, children's meals, and salads. For more sophisticate tastes, try Sesame Café, where the cuisine includes club sandwiches on focaccia, grilled chicken Caesar salads, and various Italian dishes.

Staying There

We recommend staying at the Bucks County Sheraton Hotel (800 325-3525) because it is situated right across the road from Sesame Place and because it offers a number of special packages for stays that include a free shuttle service to and from Sesame Place, a Meet & Greet at the Park with Sesame Characters, free meals for kids under 10 with an adult purchasing an entree in the Sheraton restaurant, and a free arts-and-crafts room for children with childcare workers who watch over them to give guests a child-free time, courtesy of the hotel.

There's a cozy lobby, a pub that features happy hour every afternoon starting at 4 P.M., with a changing selection of hot hors d'oeuvres and an adjoining restaurant. There is an indoor pool, fitness center, sauna/steamroom, and a coffee maker in each room. Ask for a room that overlooks Sesame Place. "Dramatic" views of little bird sitting atop the roller coaster will thrill the kids. There is also a special room for the children who love the challenge of the arcade and pin-ball machines.

The Sheraton is adjacent to an outdoor mall that has several fast food restaurants. The combination of dining at Chilis and being at Sesame Street is the stuff that kids dreams are made of.

Travel Notes

Two

and a

Half

Hours

Essex, CT

. . . one of the prettiest villages in America

WEEKEND TRIP

Getting There

Take an Amtrak train (800-USA-RAIL) from Penn Station to Old Saybrook. From there, call Essex Taxi (767-7433) to pick you up at the station and take you to the Griswold Inn. While you wait, you can browse in the adjoining antiques emporium or sip a soda at the small cafe.

Being There: Then and Now

The town of Essex was established in 1654, after the English won the area in battle from the Dutch. Its proximity to the river and its shipbuilding prowess soon made seaborne commerce central to the economy of Essex. Homes were built with widow's walks where wives could watch for the approach of their husbands' ships returning from long stretches at sea. During the Revolutionary War, the *Oliver Cromwell*—the first ship of the Continental Navy—was built in Essex.

Today, wandering through Essex conjures up peaceful feelings. This delightful village has been called "one of the prettiest in America" and was named number one in the 1996 publication of *The 100 Best Small Towns in America* by Norman Crampton. Colonial shuttered saltboxes, grand sprawling stone houses, and a smattering of New England churches are clustered on Main and Pratt Streets. Many specialty shops (some surrounded by gardens) line both sides of the road with little walks leading to a tiny mews.

Seeing and Doing

Visit the Connecticut River Museum (860-767-8269) at the end of Main Street at Steamboat Dock, where you can trace the history of the Connecticut River, the longest river in the state, once called "the great river" by the English. The museum is housed in a Victorian warehouse where spices and oils imported from the West Indies were stored. On display is a permanent exhibit of ship models, navigational, and ship-building tools, and paintings, some of which depict the burning of the ships at Essex during the War of 1812. Museum hours are Tuesday through Sunday, 10 A.M. to 5 P.M., year round.

In 1971, a group of townspeople dedicated to preserving railroad history formed the Valley Railroad Company, which now offers old-fashioned steam train rides. The steam train, built in the early 1920s, puffs and chugs and whistles, flashing its lights and ringing its bells along a century-old route, year round. It can take you to the paddlewheel boat that carries passengers past the Gillette Castle, home of the Goodspeed Opera Company, on the other side of the river.

To walk to the Valley Railroad train station, turn up Main Street, away from the river, take a left on South Main, and turn right when you reach West Avenue. Walk along

West until you get to Route 154. At your right are signs for the Valley Railroad Steam Engine Company (1 Railroad Avenue, 860-767-0103). The walk takes about a half hour, but if you're not in a hiking frame of mind or body, call Essex Taxi (767-7433) for a ride. There's also a stationary dining car where you can buy sandwiches and drinks to take on the ride, and an irresistible gift shop filled with delightful railroad paraphernalia. We bought a large steam diesel alarm clock that wakes you to clangs, whistles, and chugs.

Eating There

A complimentary continental breakfast is served in the library at the Griswold Inn to all guests from 7 to 10 A.M. every day. On Sundays, the "Gris" offers its traditional Hunt Breakfast, begun by the British when they occupied the inn during the War of 1812. Children six years old and under eat for free. Unlimited quantities of fresh fruits, chicken, fish, eggs, soufflés, and roasted meats are served from 11 A.M. to 2:30 P.M.

The Griswold Tap Room was built in 1734 as a one-room schoolhouse. In the center is a large black potbellied stove, purchased from the Goodspeed Opera House at the turn of the century. To add extra warmth, a fire crackles in a woodburning fireplace. There's even an antique popcorn machine continuously spilling out hot popcorn as you drink, eat, and enjoy the evening's entertainment that ranges from ragtime and Dixieland jazz to old sea chanties (depending on the night of the week).

Dine in the Griswold's Covered Bridge Room, built from aged timber rescued from an old bridge. It features an impressive collection of Currier and Ives steamboat prints.

Staying There

The historic Griswold Inn (203-767-1778), which first opened to the public in 1776, is the place to stay in Essex. During the War of 1812, the British Commonwealth made the Griswold its base of operations in the Connecticut Valley. The Tap Room was moved to the main inn in the late eighteenth century by a team of oxen rolling it on logs down Main Street. The inn owns and displays several outstanding collections, including rifles and handguns dating back to the fifteenth century, and a group of marine oil paintings. Guest rooms at the "Gris" are charmingly decorated with reproduction colonial wallpaper, colorful hooked rugs, and high brass beds, but the private baths, telephones, and television sets (tastefully disguised) are decidedly modern.

Southbury, CT

. . . a great resort for the whole family

WEEKEND TRIP; KID-FRIENDLY

Getting There

Bonanza buses (800-556-3815) leave from Port Authority to Southbury approximately every two hours. Your destination is the Dolce Heritage Resort. When you make reservations (203-264-8200 or 800-932-3466) you can arrange to be picked up from the station.

Seeing and Doing

During the fall and winter months, moms can relax in the Overlook Lounge (that means "overlooking the kids") near a blazing hearth while family and friends swim in an indoor pool and stretch out in a bubbling Jacuzzi. The family can play water volleyball, Ping-Pong, and racquetball. If you don't want to sweat or get wet, you can merely glance over as they engage in darts, billiards, board games, or cards in the game room, where a fire will keep you nice and toasty (we won't mention the large-screen TV; after all, this is a weekend for doing).

If it's spring or summer, you can all be outside swimming, playing tennis, biking along wooded trails, trout fishing, jogging, playing a game of horseshoes or croquet, or even golfing (there are nine- and eighteen-hole PGA-rated courses). There's even more, from horseback riding to hot-air ballooning to skiing (downhill and cross-country) to sleigh rides to horse-drawn hayrides or carriage rides, and last, but certainly not least, a quaint indoor shopping arcade featuring crafts, clothing, and little treasures for the home.

Staying There (and Eating There)

A rambling lodge surrounded by wooded trails, Heritage Inn has newly decorated guest rooms with New England–style décor. There are two restaurants on the premises. Timbers on the Green, the Inn's dining room, and Splash, an art deco bistro that serves up food and entertainment. Call for information (800-932-3466) about package deals and weekend rates.

Yes, you could spend a week here during any season and, except for golf fees, massage services, food, and beverage costs, all the activities are free.

Atlantic City, NJ

. . . not for gamblers only

DAY OR WEEKEND TRIP

Getting There

Port Authority (212-564-8484) has bus service to Atlantic City via New Jersey Transit (973-762-5100) or Academy Lines (212-964-6600). Buses leave every hour on the hour and the trip takes two and one-half hours. Ten dollars worth of quarters are given to each traveler on board compliments of the casinos. Try not to spend it all on the slot machines. Academy buses also make pick-ups at a number of other Manhattan locations (call 212-964-6600 for more information). If you prefer train travel, you can take Amtrak (800-872-7245) from Penn Station to Atlantic City.

Being There: Then and Now

Atlantic City is about more than just "hitting the casinos." It's also about the boardwalk which offers a long good-for-spring stroll past wrought-iron gas lamps and shops selling tchotchkes and saltwater taffy. You can be pushed along in an oversize white wicker pram as you could long ago, when Atlantic City was pure Americana and became the site for the Miss America Pageant. Even in winter, the boardwalk bustles with activity—you can't help but hear the sounds of unfamiliar languages spoken by visitors from all over the world. If the street names sound familiar, that's because this is the town that inspired the board game Monopoly.

Seeing and Doing

If gambling isn't your cup of tea, just wandering along the lively promenade of glittering high-rise casino hotels (each with a different theme) is a feast for the ears and eyes, with live entertainment often spilling out to the corridors and lobbies. Look for the bejeweled marble elephants that guard the swirling stone stairways to Trump's Taj Mahal. Follow the ruby-red carpeting into the Taj to the blasting brilliance of the casino halls, or stroll through the old-fashioned amusement park on the pier across from the Taj.

Huge alabaster statues beckon you into the dramatic columned halls of Caesar's Palace, where you are surrounded by staff in togas and tunics bearing trays of drinks, handing out chips, and guiding you to the blackjack tables.

Across the boardwalk from Caesar's looks to be a huge ocean liner—it's really a shopping arcade. Once known as the Million Dollar Pier, the original structure dates back to 1906 and currently houses an indoor mall, The Shops on Ocean One, with more than 100 boutiques and 25 eateries.

Eating There

You never go hungry in Atlantic City, and the prices are astonishingly low. You can almost every type of cuisine in the casino hotels along the boardwalk. Each one has several eating spots. We particularly like The Irish Pub, a turn-of-the-last-century tavern just a few steps in from the boardwalk at New York Avenue. Its walls are covered with photos of boxing champions of the '40s and '50s and you can have a good-sized ham or turkey sandwich, a mug of draft beer, and a cup of soup for about $2.99.

Staying There

Call the Chamber of Commerce (800-888-5825) for a list of accommodations, or call Accommodations Express (800-444-7666) to inquire about lodging. During the off-season days of fall and winter, many of the lavish boardwalk hotels offer rooms at moderate prices, enabling you to spend more in their downstairs casinos.

We stayed at the Atlantic Palace (800-527-8483), on New York Avenue and the Boardwalk. The rooms are large and well furnished. Ask for a high floor, overlooking the ocean—the B line is excellent. In addition to a queen-size bed with upholstered headboard, we had two pull-out couches, a four-chair dining set, and a tiny kitchen with a microwave. If you don't want to venture outside and face the evening winds, you can order in pizza or Chinese food. For us the most exciting feature of this hotel is the pink Jacuzzi in each bathroom, tucked away behind a gauze-curtained window. When you pull back the curtains, you've hit the jackpot—the most dazzling views of the sky and lights are yours to behold.

Omega Institute

RHINEBECK, NEW YORK

. . . a sleepaway camp for adults

WEEKEND TRIP

Getting There

Omega operates a special charter bus (800-944-1001) that picks up and returns participants to the Penn Station area. Alternatively, you can take a Short Line bus (800-631-8405) from Port Authority to the Beekman Arms Hotel in Rhinebeck or an Amtrak train (800-USA-RAIL) from Penn Station to Rhinecliff. An Omega shuttle van will pick you up from either station. The 800 number above will provide you with schedule and price information for all the travel choices.

Being There: Then and Now

Omega is a unique learning center where you can explore and realize your deepest self, special talents, and capacity for happiness and celebration. It's an exhilarating experience shared with remarkable people from all over the world of varying professions, talents, and ages. You can bring your kids along, too. There's a program for children ages 4 to 12 during workshop hours. And you'll probably want to return summer after summer after summer. We do.

When you arrive at Omega, once a children's camp, you may be enveloped with the same warm glow you felt as a youngster embarking on a new adventure. You won't find color wars or have to wake to reveille flag raising; but you might find workshops in African drumming and dancing presided over by Baba Olatunji; fiction and poetry writing seminars led by Marge Piercy, Billy Collins, or Sharon Olds; improvisational theater sessions with Alan Arkin. You may get to make music with renowned cellist David Darling, Rosanne Cash, Bobby McFerrin, or Meredith Monk; dance with Gabrielle Roth; discover your healing powers and spirituality with Stephen Levine and Deepak Chopra or embark on a week-long retreat with Buddhist Zen master and poet Thich Nhat Hanh.

You can sculpt statues, make pottery, draw from the left side of your brain, paint, or shoot, develop, and print photographs; all under the direction of world-renowned teachers who lead, prod, and inspire you to find your own special creative and spiritual self. Each workshop ends with an exhibition or performance that grows from the unique collaboration of minds and spirits.

Seeing and Doing

In addition to the vast array of workshops, there are ongoing yoga, tai chi, meditation, dance, and exercise classes. Sample sessions allow you to experience what various faculty members and programs have to offer. Evening activities include films, dances, musical performances, and late-night gatherings at the cafe.

The Wellness Center offers massage, bodywork, nutritional counseling, and saunas. If you're in a shopping mood, clothing, jewelry, international handicrafts, books, CDs, and tapes by Omega faculty are for sale. A tape shop can provide you with audiotapes of the workshop you just attended within hours of its completion. A cafe with indoor booths and umbrella-shaded outdoor tables sells sandwiches, salads, pasta dishes, ice cream, juices, teas, and home-baked goods every evening until 11 P.M. It's a popular hangout for just getting together and talking or singing—and there are always a couple of guitarists to oblige with accompaniment. Just walking along the wooded trails, swinging in a hammock under the trees, playing volleyball or tennis, canoeing, swimming, or lazing down by the lake are all wonderful things to do here.

For a complete catalog of courses, housing options, and travel information, call 800-862-8890 or 800-944-1001.

Eating There

Meals are served three times a day in a hilltop dining hall with many windows that look over the campus. Food is abundant, tasty, and mostly vegetarian (many of the fruits and vegetables are grown in Omega's own organic gardens), and served buffet style, with second and third helpings for the taking. You can carry your tray out to the wide terrace porch that forms a huge half circle around the building, go down the steps to the picnic tables, or spread a picnic cloth on the lawn.

Dining is always a lively experience where people share their stories and current workshop experiences and discuss the evening entertainment programs they plan to attend.

Staying There

There are cabins with private or a shared bath, dormitories, in which each sleeping space is made private by partitions, and campsites (bring your own tenting gear)—with nearby bathhouses—along the lakefront or up in the hills.

Rhinebeck, NY

. . . home of America's oldest inn

DAY OR WEEKEND TRIP

Getting There

Coach USA Short Line buses (800-631-8405) leave Port
Authority for Rhinebeck twice a day and stop in front of the
Beekman Arms Hotel. The trip takes about two hours.
Amtrak trains (800-872-7245) leave Penn Station for
Rhinecliff station several times a day. The train trip is an
hour and forty minutes, but you'll have to take a short taxi
ride from Rhinecliff to Rhinebeck. (Cabs are generally available at the station.) Although train tickets are more expensive, the beautiful train ride along the Hudson is worth it.

Being There: Then and Now

In 1715, thirty-five families fleeing persecution in the Rhine
Valley settled in this mid–Hudson valley area as tenant
farmers. They prospered, and Rhinebeck became known as
the "breadbasket of New York City."

A former stagecoach stop for weary travelers en route
from Albany to New York City, Rhinebeck was home to
Traphagen's Tavern, now the Beekman Arms Hotel. Built

two and a half centuries ago, the inn provided bed and board for travelers, and shelter for town residents against Indian attack. During the Revolutionary War, General Washington watched his troops drilling in a square from a corner window, and waited for his couriers to bring news from the battle-front; and the entire village population sought refuge at the inn following word of a possible British attack. Distinguished guests of the inn include Aaron Burr, Benedict Arnold, Alexander Hamilton, and Franklin Delano Roosevelt, who used to wind up his political campaigns on the hotel's front porch.

Seeing and Doing

The Beekman Arms Antique Barn, where more than thirty dealers sell an assortment of country collectibles and antiques, is located directly behind the main inn. There are also a number of stylish clothing and housewares shops, bookstores, and jewelry and art galleries to visit in the village. In addition, Rhinebeck hosts a variety of crafts, antiques, and horse shows throughout the year.

Eating There

An American Place Country Restaurant, located in the Beekman Arms, received an excellent rating by the *New York Times,* and serves prime rib, duck, chicken, and other regional specialties. Make a reservation for the sunny indoor garden or for the dark wood-paneled Colonial Tap Room, the center of the original inn. Also be sure to visit Schemmy's, an old-fashioned luncheonette/diner, and don't miss the London broil at Foster's.

Staying There

The Beekman Arms (4 Mill Street, on Route 9, 845-876-7077) is located in the center of the village of Rhinebeck. The oldest inn in America, it has fifty-nine guest rooms and suites, many with working fireplaces, and there's often a complimentary decanter of sherry. Down the street from the inn is the Delamater House (845-876-7080), an early example of American Capsite Gothic architecture. It was designed by one of America's first architects, Andrew Jackson Davis, and built in 1844. The parlor has a fireplace and wicker furniture. There is an adjoining courtyard and a cluster of six guesthouses, each with spacious accommodations and woodburning fireplaces.

Sag Harbor, NY

. . . charming nineteenth-century whaling village

DAY OR WEEKEND TRIP

Getting There

Take the Hampton Jitney (800-936-0449/0440) to Sag Harbor. It departs four times a day, and picks up passengers at several places in Manhattan. When you call for a reservation, ask for their current schedule, prices, and pick-up points. On a light-traffic day travel time is about two and a half hours. Comfortable seating, a restroom, and free beverages and snacks all make the bus ride quite pleasant.

Being There: Then and Now

Sag Harbor, on Gardiner's Bay at the east end of Long Island, was such a bustling port and shipbuilding center that George Washington declared it an official United States port of entry in 1789. It later became a major whaling port.

Now a National Historic District, Sag Harbor is one of the prettiest villages we visited. Restaurants, boutiques, and collectible shops are plentiful in the beautiful nineteenth-century buildings lining Main Street. We love the Variety Five-and-Dime Store, with its bright red and yellow awning shaded by gnarled old trees. Antique shops in tiny covered shacks, weathered barns, and cobbled mews are tucked away on the side streets.

Seeing and Doing

After poking through shops and lunching on fresh shrimp at a bayside restaurant, we visited the Sag Harbor Whaling and Historical Museum at Main and Garden Streets (631-725-0770), then crossed the street to the John Tremaine Library with its 60-foot dome. Later, we walked up the road to the famous Whaler's Church at East Union Street, which had its 187-foot steeple destroyed in the hurricane of 1938.

The Whaling Museum—a handsome, white-columned building, built in 1845 as a home for Captain Benjamin Hunting—features displays of ship models, tools, documents, artifacts, fashions, and even toys of the times. Sag Harbor's whaling days ended in the 1850s when the Gold Rush began, and the working people left for the hills.

Our next destination was the Custom House (631-725-0250), right across from the Whaling Museum. This wonderful shingled 1789 building, with a wide brick path leading to the front door, housed the first post office on Long Island. Furnishings and documents of the time are on display.

If you stay the entire weekend, consider taking a cruise of the Peconic and Gardiner's Bay aboard the American Beauty, a 45-foot sightseeing boat. On the 90-minute sail you pass tranquil coves and Gardiner's Island. This thousand-acre island of woodlands and meadows is home to a bird and wildlife sanctuary where one of the largest populations of osprey in the Northeast nest on specially built platforms and in tall trees.

In fine weather, you might want to rent a bike on Main Street down by the wharf and ride to the public beach.

If you love the town's charming old buildings, you can purchase a tiny replica of one at the Hadley Studio, at 97 Main Street. Mr. Hadley and his "elves" miniaturize historically important buildings of the area, and, as he puts it, "cut the Hamptons down to size." His gift shop/studio is a wonderful place for browsing.

Eating There

There are several restaurants along Main Street, leading down to the waterfront. We chose a weathered shack, part of Malloy's Dockside Restaurant, with picnic tables on the side, for a fresh seafood lunch. For dinner, we had salad and appetizers at Spinnaker's on Main Street, a cozy place with high booths and a pretty garden for outdoor dining, just a few steps from the Jitney stop. During the height of the summer season, be sure to make dinner reservations as soon as you arrive, since Spinnaker's is very popular.

Staying There

The American Hotel (631-725-3535) is a nineteenth-century brick building with white cornices and a simple front porch that looks out on Main Street. The first floor features a charming but expensive restaurant, with indoor and outdoor seating. Guest rooms are tastefully decorated with nineteenth-century furnishings.

* * *

If you spend the night in Sag Harbor, you can take in a movie on Main Street, or reserve tickets in advance to a play at the Bay Street Theatre (631-725-9100). The Bay Street Theatre has been called "a major showcase for new plays" by the *New York Times.* Tickets cost you half the price of those on Broadway.

Woodstock, NY

. . . echoes of the 1960s

DAY OR WEEKEND TRIP

Getting There

Adirondack Trailways buses (800-858-8555) leave from Port Authority and go directly to the Village Green in Woodstock. The trip takes approximately two and a half hours.

Being There: Then and Now

As the bus glides into the village of Woodstock, a handsome sign announces "Welcome to Woodstock—Colony of the Arts." Woodstock gained its reputation as a haven for individualism in 1845, when a gathering of Woodstockers disguised themselves as Indians and tarred and feathered the local rent collector.

An art colony called the Byrdcliffe Crafts Colony was established here in 1902. Between 1910 and 1916 the Woodstock Artists Association and the Maverick Concerts (America's first summer chamber music festival) were conceived by painters and musicians who were captivated by this lovely hamlet, sheltered in the valley of the Overlook and Catskill

Mountain ranges. In the years that followed (even before Woodstock gained world renown for the 1969 music festival), icons of the sixties, such as Bob Dylan and Jimi Hendrix made Woodstock their home.

In the warm months, there are flowers everywhere. And shops with names like Modern Mythology, Stone Peace, and Not Fade Away line the roads.

Seeing and Doing

You can have a wonderful weekend in Woodstock, browsing in boutiques and specialty shops, exploring galleries, and hiking country trails. The Artists Association, on Tinker Street near the village green, has information about current activities.

Just behind the Center for Photography of Woodstock (59 Tinker Street) on the banks of Tannery Brook is Tinker Village, a collection of tiny flower-laden huts. The Village's little shops sell flowers, pottery, and affordable antiques and collectibles. Tinker Street has several shops and galleries, including the Ann Leonard Gallery, featuring sculpture, paintings, graphics, and jewelry. During spring and summer, there is a large flea market every Saturday from dawn to dusk at the end of Mill House Road.

You can take a tour of the Tibetan Buddhist Monastery (tours are held at 1:30 on Saturdays and Sundays) located at 352 Meads Mountain, about two miles from the town center. The walk from town is quite scenic and lovely. After your visit to the monastery, consider heading on to Overlook Mountain to do a bit of trailblazing.

Eating There

Bistros, cafes, and cozy restaurants can be found on Tinker Street and Mill Hill Road. Blue Stone Country, across the road and "set back a bit" sells casual fare, and you can lunch in their pebbled outdoor garden. Bread Alone, 22 Mill Road, sells sandwiches on breads fresh from a wood-fired brick oven; you can buy whole loaves too. Joshua's Café, 51 Tinker Street, is famous for its four-star dining.

Staying There

We visited the very affordable Twin Gables, 73 Tinker Street (845-679-9479), about a block from where the bus pulls in. Named for its twin-gabled roofs, this bright yellow clapboard home opened its doors for lodging in the 1930s. The ambiance and furnishings of the nine guest rooms reflect the period. Some rooms have baths and some have bath shares.

The Woodstock Inn, on Mill Stream, 38 Tannery Road (845-679-8211), about two and a half blocks from the bus stop, has the ambiance of a bed-and-breakfast with motel privacy. It has eighteen units, serves a delicious breakfast, and features a classic swimming hole.

* * *

Woodstock is a state of mind, as well as a delicious place to visit—so enjoy!

Bethlehem, PA

. . . *repository of Moravian culture*

WEEKEND TRIP

Getting There

The Transbridge bus (800-962-9135) goes from Port Authority to South Bethlehem, and the stop is within walking distance of two lodging accommodations we recommend. To get to the historic district, you'll walk over the righthand side of a bridge that crosses the Lehigh River. It's a ten-minute walk with striking views of the river and the townscape. During the month of December a free trolley will transport you across the bridge.

Being There: Then and Now

In 1741 bands of Moravians (the oldest Protestant denomination) left their homes in Germany and came to the colonies as missionaries seeking converts in the New World. Settling in the lush area beside the Lehigh River and Monocacy Creek, they brought with them their devotion to industry, culture, art, education, and their abiding belief in the equality of women.

The streets are lined with well-preserved, still-occupied buildings, dating back to the eighteenth and nineteenth centuries. On Main Street, the evening lamplight from Victorian street lamps glows softly upon the brick-and-slate patterned walkways, hitching posts, and stone watering troughs.

Seeing and Doing

As you cross the bridge into the historic district, you see the bell-shaped tower of the Central Moravian Church on the corner of Main and Church Streets. To your right is the fieldstone Single Brethren House, erected in 1748, where single men lived before they married. George Washington made it a hospital during the Revolutionary War. Most of the other old buildings are on Church Street, but make your first stop the Bethlehem Chamber of Commerce at 509 Main Street (610-867-3788). There you can purchase a booklet with a self-guided tour about the two city blocks between Broad and Church Streets that spans three centuries. Highlights include the Single Sisters House, built in 1772, the Moravian College, and the five-story log Moravian Museum of Bethlehem, the oldest structure in the district. Also of note is the eighteenth-century industrial area below Main Street alongside Monocacy Creek. Here, a small limestone building constructed in 1762, and now a national historic landmark, housed the first municipal water system in the American colonies. The Kemerer Museum of Decorative Arts, on New Street, has rooms of colonial and Victorian furnishings and the largest collection of Bohemian glassware in the States.

For shopping, Main and Broad Streets have beautiful shops—vast, airy spaces full of exquisite clothing, jewelry, antiques, and remarkable collectibles.

As you can imagine, Bethlehem goes all out for Christmas. The tradition began on Christmas Eve in 1741, when a small group of Moravian settlers celebrated the holiday in the tiny log cabins that were their first homes in this country. Singing and carrying lighted candles, they named their new village Bethlelem. Today, the entire town glows with sparkling trees and candlelit windows, while a ninety-one-foot-high shining "North Star" atop South Mountain, towers over Bethlehem and can be seen for many miles. If you want to visit Bethlehem during the Christmas season, you have to make hotel reservations at least eight months in advance.

Bethlehem is also a lively place to be in summer, especially in August, when the city plays host to the weeklong Musik Fest.

Eating There

Since 1760, the Sun Inn at 564 Main Street (610-974-9451) has welcomed such famous guests as Benjamin Franklin, George and Martha Washington, Samuel and John Adams, Ethan Allen, and the Marquis de Lafayette. Restored to its authentic Moravian architectural style, its first floor is now a museum, with costumed guides who recount its rich and colorful history. On the second floor, you can dine in an eighteenth-century atmosphere.

The Moravian Book Shop, 428 Main Street, which carries books of every age, size, and description and has a gift shop, features a small serve-yourself restaurant. The fare is light gourmet, delicious, and reasonably priced. Ana Mia, on Fourth Street, is a beautiful Italian restaurant in a former home. To get there, walk up New Street along Third.

Staying There

Just a block from the little gray trailer that houses the South Bethlehem bus station is the Comfort Suites Motel (800-228-5150), a clean, contemporary complex of 124 newly decorated suites complete with microwave ovens, refrigerators, and cable TV with free HBO. Rates are reasonable. To get there, turn left from the bus stop and walk half a block to Third Street, turn left again, and the hotel is on the next corner.

For a posh overnight stay (great for sharing with friends) we recommend the Sayre Mansion Inn (610-882-2100). You can walk there from the bus station, following the same path as the one to Comfort Suites, then continue up the hill to 250 Wyandotte Street. The walk takes about five minutes, or you can call a cab from the bus station. The inn was once the home of Robert Heysham Sayre, an industrialist who shared it with his wife and eleven children. Sayre Mansion has two enchanting parlor rooms, each with its own cozy fireplace, and nineteen antique-filled guest rooms with private baths and modern amenities.

Bethlehem's historic district has the flavor of a small European town. Being there is like visiting another country. It was one of our most enjoyable excursions.

If you'd enjoy staying in the heart of the historic district, a night or two at the Radisson Hotel Bethlehem, 437 Main Street (610-625-5000) can be an enchanting experience. This grand hotel has been restored to its original 1922 opulence, reflected in its handsome lobby, spiral staircases, and ornate balconies. The floor-to-ceiling palladium windows look out upon a storybook Main Street. Guest rooms are painted in rich hues of navy and gold and offer spectacular views of Bethlehem. The hotel is also home to The Colonnade Steakhouse, a world-class restaurant, and a tap room where lunch and light dinners are served daily.

When making reservations, be sure to tell the reservationist that you will want to have the hotel van pick you up and bring you back to the South Bethlehem bus station at the end of your stay.

Three

to

Four
Hours

(EXTENDED WEEKEND TRIPS)

Jim Thorpe, PA

... America's little Switzerland in the foothills of the Poconos

WEEKEND TRIP

Getting There

Susquehanna Trailways (800-692-6314) goes directly from Port Authority to the town of Jim Thorpe. The trip takes about three hours and fifteen minutes each way. Although the ride is long, the views, when entering Pennsylvania are magnificent. You pass rolling farmlands, tranquil lakes, sweeping mountain ranges and little towns where time has stood still. For this trip, we suggest you get a seat on the right side of the bus toward the back end of the window so as to have the widest view.

When you leave the bus, turn left on Broadway and just a few more steps will take you right to your hotel, if you've chosen to stay at the Inn at Jim Thorpe. A few more blocks to your left will bring you to several charming B&Bs along West Broadway.

Being There; Now:

Broadway, a winding hilly street set against the backdrop of the majestic Pocono Mountains, is lined with exquisite Victorian buildings adorned with fanciful architectural features such as turrets, spires, cupolas, and mansard roofs. It was once known as millionaire's row because thirteen very wealthy men, who gained their money and their prominence during the industrial revolution, made their homes there.

The village of Jim Thorpe was also known as "little Switzerland" or the Switzerland of America. In autumn, the mountains are awash in the vivid golds, oranges and scarlets of the season . . . a truly stunning vision to behold.

Then

The town of Jim Thorpe has had several names during its history, which dates back to 1815. At that time it was known as Coalville and was laid out along the Lehigh River. Merchant entrepreneurs from the area formed the Lehigh Coal and Navigation company (later, the switchback railroad, was built to carry coal, as well) to develop the transport of anthracite coal via the Lehigh and Delaware River to large Eastern cities like New York and Philadelphia.

Immigrants from Wales, Ireland, and England came to work here. "Coalville," which later was changed to Mauch Chunk (Indian for black bear) was one of the very first towns where the industrial revolution began. An era of great prosperity from the 1870s through the 1920s brought visitors in great droves. This period of wealth endowed the village with a remarkable legacy of both simple and grand residential buildings.

After 1920, when the coal industry began its decline, the town entered a time of economic depression. The town fathers, wanting to elevate the village to its former standing, eventually united Mauch Chunk and East Mauch Chunk to form one borough called Jim Thorpe. The time was 1954 and Jim Thorpe, champion of the 1912 Olympics and considered one of the greatest athletes of the 20th century, had died in his hometown in Oklahoma. Because of financial difficulties, he was not able to receive the kind of burial his wife felt he deserved. So in exchange for Jim Thorpe's name and a proper memorial, she had his body buried in Mauch Chunk . . . now to be called Jim Thorpe (a town he had never set foot in).

The new name stirred interest in the village and a second wave of tourism began, creating a second time of prosperity for this hamlet in the foothills of the Poconos.

Seeing and Doing

Today, the town of Jim Thorpe continues to be an idyllic place to visit because of its great natural beauty and because of the variety of ways it offers to spend your time. You can shop, museum hop, take a train ride through the mountains, ride a bike along the Lehigh River or even mountain bike into the wooded hills. Shops and emporiums in this village are chock full of treasures from folk art to collections of the exotic and bizarre.

If you love dolls that look like real babies and children, stop in at "Hello Dolly" at the corner of Race Street and Broadway. While you are there, ask the proprietor to show you the underground stream that rushes underneath the shop.

What we found especially exciting is the Mauch Chunk five-and-dime on Broadway. Offering the same items you used to be able to buy at Woolworth's, Mauch Chunk's prices are really low and their stock ranges from colorful regional tin roosters and artistically crafted lamps and candleholders to great underwear buys and country placemats with an array of healing capsules, creams, oils, herbs, and vitamins for all your health needs at $1 a piece.

Several museums in town celebrate and educate visitors about the extraordinary history of the town. The first place to visit is the Mauch Chunk Museum and Cultural Center at 41 West Broadway. Housed in the former St. Paul's Methodist Church, constructed in 1843, this building is a fine example of Victorian ecclesiastical architecture. Once inside this simple museum, you will find exhibits of painting, photographs, furnishings and maps depicting Mauch Chunk's horse-and-buggy days.

Asa Packer, a wealthy entrepreneur from Mauch Chunk provided the funds needed to build the Lehigh Valley Railroad in 1851. It eventually ran for 650 miles from New York State to the New Jersey seaboard. A great philanthropist, Packer founded Lehigh University in Bethlehem, Pa. and was the Democratic nominee for President of the United States in 1868.

Overlooking the Jim Thorpe historic district, the Asa Packer Mansion, reconstructed in 1861, is a proud Victorian with wraparound porches and a turreted roof. Set in the Gothic motif, its interiors are filled with handcrafted woodwork, stained-glass windows and furnishings characteristic of the American Empire style. From Memorial Day to the end of October, the Packer House is open seven days a week.

Designed by Richard Upjohn, the country's leading architect in the field of religious construction, St. Marks Episcopal Church at 21 Race Street was dedicated in November of 1869 and designated in 1987 as a national historic landmark. It was Upjohn's last and most fascinating work.

The church of gothic design has an interior laid out in the form of a cross, tiffany stained glass windows, graceful statuary and an altar of white marble. It is considered an architectural treasure.

The handsome stone houses on Race Street adjacent to St. Marks Church are a fine example of the workers' homes during the Industrial Revolution. This section of Race Street can be considered a museum without walls.

Built in 1871, the Old Jail Museum at 128 West Broadway contains 28 cells, the warden's living quarters and 16 eerie dungeons. The Jail became famous between 1877 and 1879 when seven men accused of being Molly Maguires, a notorious gang, were hung in the gallows for murder. One of their handprints can still be seen on the wall of cell 17 today.

Blue Mountain Sporting Goods store (800-599-4421) at Race & Susquehanna Streets offers an opportunity to bike ten to twenty-five miles outside the town of Jim Thorpe. When you rent your bike, they provide helmets, maps and a shuttle service to a spot of your choice along the Lehigh River. You can coast along the flat path way on the riverbank back into Jim Thorpe. Although this project was not actually designed for public transportation travelers, it suits our needs and those of our readers (you) perfectly! Blue Mountain rents all the equipment you will need for mountain biking.

Eating There

How long has it been since you've heard of a 24-ounce steak for $12.95? Ever? Well, these beautifully cooked steaks with fresh salad and baked potato can be yours every evening in the Steak & Ale House at the Hotel Switzerland on Broadway & Hazard Square just across the street from the bus stop. Just around the corner from the Hotel Switzerland is the Sunrise Diner. Established in 1951, this tiny, shiny silver classic serves traditional meat and potato platters for dinner and a variety of sandwiches for lunch. Prices are almost as inexpensive as they were at the time it opened. We were able to buy a full-course dinner for $5.00 and had to refrain from the newly baked pies just out of the oven, their crusts brimming over the top with fresh fruit and dollops of whipped cream. On the corner of Race Street at 111 Broadway, step onto the porch of a striking Victorian building and you'll find yourself in "Through the Looking Glass Café." Inside is a classic plant-filled Victorian parlor with a bay window, charming cafe tables and chairs, cast iron mantle, unique wall carvings and tiffany lamps. The cafe serves a variety of homemade soups and sandwiches, along with gourmet coffees.

Staying There

In 1849, when coal was king and America's second oldest railroad was running, the town of Mauch Chunk was America's second favorite vacation spot next to Niagara Falls. At that time, The American Hotel—now called The Inn at Jim Thorpe—opened its doors. This 39-room inn is a wonderful link to America's bygone days. Its Victorian style lobby glows with red silk lampshades and a flickering fireplace. Paintings and old photographs depict this graceful New Orleans style building as a backdrop for passing horses and buggies and a few brand new "horseless carriages."

Choose from standard rooms to suites complete with Jacuzzis. Ask for one in the back of the inn that looks out on the mountains and the Asa Packer mansion. The inn has a variety of wonderful packages. Be sure to inquire about them when making your reservations. A delicious continental breakfast is served every morning. For reservations and any other information, call 800-329-2599.

There are several charming B&Bs on Broadway and West Broadway. Among them are the Victoria Ann at 68 Broadway (888-241-4460) and Rendon House at 80 Broadway (570-325-5515).

We want to remind you again about the Hotel Switzerland (570-325-4563). Founded in 1830, this homey inn at Broadway & Hazard Square is the oldest commercial building in town. It has nine very pretty rooms fully restored with cozy wallpaper, lace curtains and vintage furnishings. All look out to one of the majestic Pocono Mountains. Who could ask for anything more?

Mystic, CT

... historic seaport with tall ships and

soaring church spires

WEEKEND TRIP

Getting There

Amtrak trains (800-USA-RAIL) go directly from Grand Central Station to Mystic. It's a three-hour trip through lovely scenery and the train stops right at the edge of downtown.

Being There: Then and Now

Founded in the seventeenth century, the town of Mystic quickly became a shipbuilding center. Now drawing visitors from all across the country, this small seaport city satisfies a yearning to experience America's nautical past.

At the Mystic Seaport Museum (860-572-0761), you can explore four magnificent tall ships, from the crews' quarters below the decks to the huge masts above. The museum's holdings also include hundreds of small boats and a number of historic shops and houses.

Amble through an old-time grocery store, a school-house, and a printer's shop. On display are maritime artifacts including majestic ship figureheads and nautical instruments, as well as toys that kept children happy during long-ago journeys over the sea. Be sure to spend some time in the planetarium, where you can learn about the wonders of celestial navigation.

Seeing and Doing

You need at least an extended weekend to sample all of Mystic's offerings. To reach Main Street, walk over the charming Bascule drawbridge. The downtown area has many historic homes, antique emporiums, boutiques, interesting gift shops, and restaurants. You can take half- and full-day sails on the Charlotte Anne, a completely refurbished schooner built in 1888, from Steamboat Wharf in downtown Mystic in the spring and summer (860-536-0416).

Old Mystic Village, on Cogan Boulevard, is a half-hour walk from downtown. This charming replica of a New England village, complete with white clapboard church, is a shopping complex of stores selling an assortment of goods.

Besides the Seaport Museum there's the Mystic Aquarium (860-572-5955), featuring fabulous performances by dolphin, seals, and whales. If you're visiting from April to October, a trolley can transport you from downtown Mystic to the aquarium (as well as to other attractions); at other times of year you need to take a taxi since the trolley doesn't run and it's at least a four-mile hike.

For more information and a comprehensive walking tour of the village's historic sites, call the Mystic Tourist Information Center (860-536-1641).

Eating There

There are so many pubs, cafes, and fine restaurants on Main Street that you're sure to find a few that will especially appeal to you. Most feature seafood specialties, with an abundant selection of lobster, shrimp, and crabmeat entrées and appetizers. You may want a slice at Mystic Pizza (of movie fame!). The pizza is excellent, even if Julia Roberts doesn't serve you. At The Whaler's Inn, on South Main, you can dine outdoors under a huge open tent in spring and summer.

Staying There

Mystic has many overnight lodging options. Call the Chamber of Commerce (203-536-8559) for a complete list. We stayed at The Whaler's Inn, 20 East Main Street (800-243-2588) because of its charm and proximity to the historic downtown area and the railroad station. A three-story clapboard "home," its lobby resembles a cozy parlor room, and its guest rooms are immaculate and pleasantly furnished with large, comfortable beds. Ask about weekend packages.

*   *   *

You might also like to spend a couple of hours in Stonington, an old whaling village, just a short cab ride away. Rows of Victorian homes and sea captain's houses line the winding narrow streets. It is hard to imagine that this serene little whitewashed town has changed at all since the seventeenth century, when it lured luminaries such as James Whistler, Stephen Vincent Benét, and Edgar Allan Poe.

Baltimore, MD

. . . glorious Inner Harbor and Fells Point—
a delightful fishing village

WEEKEND TRIP; KID-FRIENDLY

Getting There

Amtrak trains (800-USA-RAIL) go directly to Baltimore from Penn Station. The ride takes about three and a half hours. Greyhound (800-231-2222) and Trailways buses (800-343-9999) depart for Baltimore from Port Authority. Although the ride takes about an hour longer than the train, it costs less. Whichever option you choose, you need to take a taxi from the station in Baltimore to your hotel (there are always plenty waiting at both stations).

Being There: Then and Now

Baltimore is a city of diverse ethnic neighborhoods. In the mid-1900s, many immigrants who passed through Baltimore stayed and found work in the canneries and on the railroads. They lived in Baltimore's well-known row houses, with their characteristic scrubbed-white marble steps, which were built at low cost so that workers could own their own homes. From these humble beginnings, Baltimore has become a town with sophisticated neighborhoods. Writer Anne Tyler, filmmaker Barry Levinson, and jazz greats Billie Holiday and Eubie Blake have all made their homes in Baltimore.

Seeing and Doing

Baltimore has much to offer visitors, and you'll want to return to see and do more. Start with two of our favorite destinations—the exciting Inner Harbor and the delightful historic district of Fells Point.

The Inner Harbor has come a long way since the British shelled its Ft. McHenry during the War of 1812 and inspired Francis Scott Key to write the *Star-Spangled Banner*. Today this area has been renovated into a magnificent public promenade and waterfront plaza. Luxurious hotels, glass-enclosed restaurants, and shops surround the promenade, and it's the setting for festivals all summer long. Two great attractions for children, The Maryland Science Center (410-685-9225) and the National Aquarium (410-576-3800), which boasts the biggest shark tank in America, anchor the Inner Harbor. The harbor bustles with paddleboats, water taxis, cruise boats, and a tall ship. By the way, the Inner Harbor is within easy walking distance of Baltimore's gorgeous new retro baseball stadium.

After enjoying the activities on the Inner Harbor, board a bright red trolley on Light Street and travel up elegant Charles Street getting off and on at different locations as you please. This hilly street is lined with art galleries and boutiques leading to Mt. Vernon Square, a park ringed by splendid mansions.

Water taxis go back and forth between Fells Point and the Inner Harbor. A five-minute ride costs about $2.00, but you can also take a trolley. Fells Point is a charming waterfront community of quaint row houses along cobblestone streets. It is also home to many restaurants, art galleries, antique shops, boutiques, collectible emporiums, and bookstores, as well as the occasional tin-ceilinged bar once patronized by shipbuilders, seamen, and merchants during the days when clipper ships and schooners were built in the local shipyards.

Walk along beautiful Ann Street and note the one-of-a-kind decorative screen doors on many of the homes. The scenic paintings on the doors prevent passersby from seeing in, while the screens permit the cool river breezes to circulate inside—a big help to the sweltering inhabitants before the days of fans and air conditioners.

Eating There

Fells Point restaurants include charming bistros, cafes, and century-old taverns. The seafood featured in many restaurants is caught from Maryland's famous Chesapeake Bay. One of the best-known seafood spots is Bertha's, at 734 South Broadway (410-327-5795), a cozy tavern that boasts the town's largest variety of dishes prepared with mussels. You can indulge in mussels with anchovy, tomato, and garlic butter; with spinach, tarragon, and garlic sauce; or with sour cream and scallions. Another well-known seafood spot is Francie's Restaurant & Row Bar, 1629 Thomas Street, with its wide decks stretching along the water. The Wharf Rat Bar, 801 South Ann Street (410-276-9034), is an active, colorful hangout, featuring twenty-seven varieties of beer on tap. You can get a great cup of coffee at the Daily Grind Coffee House, 1720 Thames Street (410-558-0399), in a low-lit, spacious setting decorated with local art.

The Inner Harbor has a wide variety of restaurants, as well as a huge indoor food court, featuring many different cuisines plus fresh crabs, oysters, and clams at Phillips, Baltimore's most famous seafood restaurant.

Staying There

Fells Point: Ann Street Bed and Breakfast, at 804 South Ann Street (410-342-5883), is comprised of a pair of eighteenth-century restored colonial houses complete with fireplaces, private baths, colonial pine furnishings, and a lovely garden where breakfast is served. The Inn at Henderson's Wharf, 1000 Fell Street (800-522-2088 or 410-522-7777) was formerly a nineteenth-century tobacco warehouse. Situated right on the waterfront, this gracious bed and breakfast has its own dock where a water taxi can pick you up and later return you to your front door. The rooms, decorated in English country style, look out on a lush garden with splashing fountains. Admiral Fell Inn, 888 South Broadway (410-522-7377), is located near the water's edge and offers rooms with Federal Period furnishings.

Inner Harbor: High-rise hotels, such as the Marriott, Sheraton, and Hyatt surround the Inner Harbor. A smaller, elegant, European-style hotel, the Harbor Court, 550 Light Street (800-824-0076), is famous for its library, which contains books from all over the world.

Kripalu Center, Lenox

. . . health and yoga retreat in a breathtaking setting

WEEKEND TRIP

Getting There

Bonanza buses (800-556-3815) leave Port Authority for Lenox, Massachusetts, three times a day. The bus ride takes just under four hours. A Kripalu shuttle will pick you up at the Lenox bus stop. Request the shuttle service when you call to make your Kripalu reservations (800-741-7353); it costs $5 each way.

Being There: Then and Now

A former Jesuit seminary on a 300-acre wooded site in the Berkshire Mountains (adjacent to Tanglewood), this sprawling four-story brick building was built in 1957 and laid out by Frederick Law Olmsted.. From the road you see a simple, if not Spartan, hilltop red-brick structure, but from inside if you look out of any window—and they are vast in size and number—you will see magnificent scenescapes of gardens and lakefront, and ranges of green-carpeted mountains spilling up into endless sky.

In this exquisite natural setting, Kripalu is a sanctuary where you can relax your body, calm your mind, and strengthen yourself inside and outside.

Seeing and Doing

The activities at Kripalu are designed to bring you to new levels of vibrant health, peace of mind, and spiritual attunement. Skilled instructors guide you in yoga, meditation, relaxation, moving on (releasing past; embracing new possibilities), transforming stress, and healing. Classes and workshops also include African drumming, mask-making, dreamwork, painting, writing, dancing, singing, and chanting.

You can attend many types of daily workshops or just read or reflect in the deep-cushioned couches and chairs. Or write at the small wicker desks that furnish the tree-filled sunroom (open 24 hours), walk on the trails, relax in the whirlpools and saunas, or browse in the Kripalu Shop among a wide selection of books, videotapes, audiotapes, bodycare items, natural-fiber clothing, handcrafted jewelry, crystals, candles, and delicious snacks.

Eating There

Meals are served cafeteria style three times a day in a large, bright country dining hall, where you eat at long wooden tables. You can chat with other guests at lunch and dinner, but breakfast is designated as a silent meal to provide tranquil time to get ready for the day's activities.

The delectable food is strictly vegetarian: Meals are rich in protein and fiber and moderately low in fats and sweeteners—fresh vegetables and homebaked breads abound. The evening meal might be luscious lasagna (with or without cheese), a tasty curry, hearty squash-and-potato stew, or one of a variety of Mexican-style combinations. You can eat to your heart's content and even learn to love tofu— we did.

Staying There

Accommodations range from dormitory rooms with clean, comfortable bunk beds to more spacious rooms furnished in white wicker with queen size and twin beds. There are several large, immaculate bathrooms to share on every floor. Only a few rooms have private baths.

*　*　*

Open throughout the year, Kripalu is a place for all seasons. In the fall, the foliage is magnificent, and in summer you can swim and sun by the lake.

For current information, program schedule, and catalog, call 800-741-7353. Rates include workshops, program activities, meals, and accommodations.

Lenox, MA

. . . cultural center in the foothills
of the Berkshire Mountains

WEEKEND TRIP

Getting There

Bonanza buses (800-556-3815) leave from Port Authority for
Lenox three times a day, arriving just across the road from Lenox
Town Hall. The nearly four-hour trip from Manhattan takes you
through hilly farmland, low stone walls, and covered bridges
along one of the most scenic routes in America—Connecticut's
Route 7. The bus makes stops in the picturesque New England
villages of Kent, Sheffield, Great Barrington, and Stockbridge.

Being There: Then and Now

Dubbed as the "inland Newport," Lenox served as a retreat
and summer home for the wealthy and for many literary
greats during the mid-nineteenth century. A community of
extravagant summer "cottages" sprang up, along with
a multitude of cultural activities. Longfellow, Melville,
Hawthorne, Henry Adams, and Edith Wharton gathered
here to write. All described the beauty of Lenox, its hilly ter-
rain, and the spectacular Berkshire Mountains.

Today, Lenox is the site of a variety of cultural pursuits, particularly during mild weather. It is the summer home of the Boston Symphony Orchestra at Tanglewood and of Jacob's Pillow, which features some of the finest dance in the country. In spring and fall the scenery is gorgeous, and in winter, several nearby ski slopes are popular destinations.

Seeing and Doing

Once the crowds for the music and dance festivals have retreated, a serenity fills the air and there is still enough activity to engage a curious traveler. Take your pick from chamber music concerts, high teas, cross-country skiing, birdwatching treks, lolling about in an old-fashioned inn, reading under the green banker's lamps at the famous Lenox Library, or browsing through the boutiques and collectibles shops that line Church and Walker Streets. Concepts of Art, 65 Church Street (413-637-4845), carries a unique line of Judaica, including books, paintings, sculptures, jewelry, and other objets d'art.

Although some inns are closed during the off-season (winter and early spring), room rates are lower at these times. Lenox is a town of antiques shops, clothing stores, galleries, churches, historic buildings, and wooded parks. You can rent a bike, a canoe, in-line skates, snowshoes, skis, tennis racquets, and roller blades at the Sport Store on Main Street (413-637-3353)—they have information on bicycle routes, hiking trails, and guided outdoor tours. At the Chamber of Commerce, also on Main Street, pick up a copy of *Walking Through Lenox History*.

Housed in a landmark building with domed ceilings and marble walls, the Lenox Library on Main Street is open all week long and on weekends till 7 P.M. High-backed wing chairs are clustered about a fireplace in a reading room that features a wide selection of old books and magazines, as well as contemporary titles. Be sure to stop by—it is the most beautiful library we have ever seen.

You can walk or bicycle over to the Mount, where Edith Wharton wrote some of her most important novels (*Ethan Frome* was based on a sledding accident that took place in Lenox at the bottom of Court House Hill). Perched on a knoll of landscaped gardens that Wharton created and called her "outdoor rooms," this grand house was designed by the writer in 1901. To reach the Mount, walk down Kimble Street to where it meets Route 7A.

Eating There

Lenox has a variety of restaurants, some sophisticated and others simple and casual. The Church Street Cafe (65 Church, 413-637-2745) located in a white clapboard house, specializes in Italian cuisine. We had an assortment of appetizers, along with a carafe of merlot and a basket of home-baked bread. The Roseborough Grill (71 Church, 413-637-2700) is a friendly country cafe with indoor and outdoor tables, serving New England and continental menus. The Church Street Deli (37 Church) features hot sandwiches, chili, and French onion soup as well as bagels with cream cheese and lox.

Staying There

We stayed at the Gables Inn at 81 Walker Street (413-637-3416). Just a few steps from the bus stop, it's a beautifully restored hundred-year-old Queen Anne Berkshire "cottage" that was the home of Edith Wharton's mother-in-law. Wharton spent two years writing short stories in its library. A stay here is a visit to the Gilded Age: You'll find damask wallpaper, thick Oriental rugs, shaded Victorian lamps, a collection of porcelain dolls, wood-burning fireplaces, and plush curved-back couches upholstered with vivid floral brocades. Bookshelves line the parlor walls, and there's always an open bottle of port and crystal glasses, so help yourself. Many guest rooms have canopied four-poster beds and fireplaces; most have private baths. There are no televisions or telephones in the rooms, although there is a large TV in the main parlor.

The Gables serves a full breakfast of pancakes or waffles, eggs, juice, homebaked muffins, melon, and tea or coffee in the lavish dining room. Leaded floor-to-ceiling windows look out over the pool and tennis courts. Classical music plays softly in the background.

We also visited the Gateway's Inn, a few doors past the Gables, at 51 Walker Street (413-637-2532). Built in 1912 as a summer home for Harley Procter of Procter & Gamble, some say the inn's design is reminiscent of a bar of Ivory Soap. The rooms have antique furnishings and private baths, and some have working fireplaces. During his Tanglewood performances, Arthur Fiedler, the late conductor of the Boston Pops, spent many summers in the spacious suite that now bears his name. For more than fourteen years, the inn's restaurant has received Mobil's four-star rating—only four other New England restaurants can lay claim to this honor.

Built in 1771, the Village Inn, just around the corner at 16 Church Street (413-637-0020), has thirty-two guest rooms furnished with country antiques; some with working fireplaces and canopy beds. All have private baths. Its restaurant serves breakfast, traditional afternoon English tea, and candlelit dinners in summer and fall. The downstairs Tavern features English ales, draught beer, and a light menu.

Stockbridge, MA

... *welcome to Norman Rockwell country*

WEEKEND TRIP

Getting There

Bonanza buses (800-556-3815) out of Port Authority stop right in front of the Red Lion Inn. Although the ride takes four hours, the scenery (especially on Route 7, which begins in Connecticut) is spectacular, the bus is air conditioned, and the seats are comfortable.

Being There: Then and Now

In the mid-1800s the Housatonic Railway came through Stockbridge, and wealthy families, discovering the beauty of the area, built lavish summer "cottages," there and in nearby Lenox. A literary colony formed, followed by theater, classical music, and dance programs that have continued up to today and now draw people to the Berkshires from all over the United States.

Many visitors stay at the Red Lion Inn. At one time, the site was the home of the Mahkeenac Indian tribe. Upon their departure, Colonialist Silas Pepoon established the Red Lion. By 1773, the Red Lion tavern was a stagecoach stop and the village center for discussing politics. At a major convention held at the tavern on July 6, 1774, colonists resolved to boycott British goods in protest of the five Intolerable Acts, which Britain had passed in response to the Boston Tea Party. In 1896, the original Red Lion Inn burned to the ground but was rebuilt and reopened the following year with few changes.

Staying There

If we were to daydream about the perfect country inn, we couldn't come any closer than the Red Lion Inn at 30 Main Street (413-298-5545). It's splendid and simple at the same time. Red-carpeted steps lead to a wide veranda, dotted with rockers and wicker chairs. Oak doors are opened for you by uniformed attendants as you step into a lobby of exquisite Victorian charm. Oriental rugs, plump period sofas and chairs all reflect the grandeur of the times. A brass "bird-cage" elevator takes you to your floor, where long carpeted corridors lead to simply furnished rooms. The hotel has added some modern amenities and there is a library on the third floor, a courtyard dining area, and a swimming pool (some modern amenities do nothing to detract from the nineteenth-century atmosphere).

Call the Red Lion for room rates and reservations. Some small rooms, with bathrooms down the hall, go for a moderate rate.

Seeing and Doing

When you've done enough rocking on the old front porch and inhaled enough fresh mountain air, you'll be ready for the wonderful shopping in Stockbridge. The original Yankee Candle makes its home on Main Street, and there are numerous collectibles shops and boutiques all around town.

Just across the street at the tiny Chamber of Commerce, you can pick up literature about Stockbridge and look out on the streetscape that was the setting for Norman Rockwell's famous painting *Main Street Stockbridge at Christmastime* (prints can be bought in many shops around town). Rockwell, whose studio was in the center of town, made Stockbridge his home for the last twenty-five years of his life.

In 1986, the studio was moved to the site of the Rockwell Museum, about two miles away. The museum and studio are set on thirty-six hilly acres overlooking the Housatonic River. At the front desk of the Red Lion you can ask for a little map to show you a simple way to walk there. Biking is also an option.

Down the road from the Rockwell Museum is the Berkshire Botanical Gardens. Founded in 1934, it is one of the oldest horticulture centers in the U.S. The gardens are open from May through October and will treat you to a wonderland of spring and summer blooms.

If you're up for a hike through glacial boulders, walk over to the Ice Glen area—a few blocks from Main Street—at the end of Park Street. Cross the footbridge over the Housatonic River and follow the challenging marked trail up the slopes through an ancient scene of glaciers, where ice crystals can be seen even in summer. The summit of your exploration is Laura's Tower, from which you can see Mt. Everette to the southwest, the Catskills of New York to the west, and Vermont's Green Mountains to the north. The hike can take several hours, so be sure to bring drinks and munchies for the journey.

For a fabulous sidetrip from Stockbridge, we suggest an expedition into Great Barrington, another beautiful New

England town with a little more urban flair—it has sophisticated boutiques, antique stores, and sushi bars. To get to
Great Barrington, you can take a local bus that stops in front
of the Chamber of Commerce (right across the street from
the Red Lion). The trip takes about a half an hour and runs
every hour. Ask the driver to let you off near Railroad Street.

We loved ambling around the fabulous boutiques and
other chic shops on Castle and Railroad Streets. The Yellow
Bookshop on Main Street was especially good for browsing. We
did not stay overnight in Great Barrington; however, if you
want information about lodgings in town, call 800-237-5747.

Eating There

The dining options at the Red Lion Inn include the elegant
main dining room, where jackets are required for gentlemen
and no blue jeans may be worn at the evening meal; the rustic Widow Bingham's Tavern is perfect for intimate and
more casual dining; and The Lion's Den, where we enjoyed
lighter fare for dinner at lighter prices, offers entertainment.
There are several restaurants on Main Street, and we had a
delicious lunch in the garden of Teresa's (413-298-5465),
which was the original "Alice's Restaurant," famous for the
movie and song of the same name.

*   *   *

Like the other trips in this three-to-four hour category,
Stockbridge makes a delightful extended weekend or mid-
week trip and can be visited any time of year. You need to
make plans well in advance, however, if you'd like to visit
during the busy summer and fall foliage seasons.

Lancaster, PA

...center of Amish life and culture; perfect for a long weekend

WEEKEND TRIP

Getting There

Amtrak trains (800-872-7245) leave from Penn Station for Lancaster five times a day; the trip takes three-and-a-half hours. Capital Trailways buses leave from Port Authority (800-333-8444) for Lancaster several times a day and that ride also takes about three-and-a-half hours, however the bus fare is considerably less expensive than the train. We suggest staying at the Hotel Brunswick (800-233-0182) at Chestnut Street and Queen Street because of its proximity to the city's historic landmarks, the bus station, and the train terminal. (A taxi to the hotel from the bus or train is under $5.00—call Friendly Taxi at 800-795-3278).

When you register, be sure to ask the desk clerk for a city bus schedule to White Horse—you may need it for your later adventures. You can also pick a schedule up at the corner of Queen and Chestnut streets at the Red Rose Transit Company, just a block from the hotel.

Being There: Then and Now

Settled in the early 1700s by Swiss Mennonites, Lancaster County soon became home to a large population of Amish, inspired by William Penn's promise of religious freedom and good farmland.

The Amish called themselves "plain people" and they try to keep their lives as simple as when they first came to this country. No modern devices, no electricity, no motor driven vehicles, no indoor telephones. Horses and buggies are the only means of travel.

Seeing and Doing

Twisting cobblestone paths lead from the Hotel Brunswick up to Central Market. Dating back to the 1730s, this is the oldest covered market in the nation. It has been splendidly restored with distinctive towers, gas lamps, and red brick facades. Inside is a bountiful array of homegrown produce from the surrounding farms, as well as jams and jellies, breads and pastries, meats and cheeses, and crafts. We were happy to see the ethnic variety of foods, ranging from kosher baked goods and hummus to stuffed grape leaves. Open from 6 A.M. to 4:30 P.M. weekdays, the market closes at 2 P.M. Saturdays and is closed Sundays.

Meandering on brick roads through courtyards and alleyways, you come upon pitching posts still used by Lancaster's Amish for their horses and buggies and by the city's mounted police. Shops and galleries appear at every turn selling everything from country crafts to sophisticated art and sculpture.

Leaving Central Market, take a right on King Street and follow King until it intersects with Prince Street. There you see the Fulton Opera House, a national historic landmark built in 1852, and currently home to several popular theater companies. Also on Prince is the Angry Young & Poor Punk Record & Clothing Shop. A few doors down is a bookshop specializing in hard-to-find books. Although it's closed Sundays, you can browse through outdoor shelves and purchase a book by the honor system, dropping a dollar or two into the mail slot at the bottom of the door.

Country Jaunts

The main reason most travelers come to Lancaster Country is to visit the quaint villages and farms nestled in the Amish countryside. Pay attention to the details of this section since getting around without a car can be tricky and, according to the advice of a number of locals, "just can't be done." Well it can. We researched and designed original and (we think) ingenious ways to explore the area without a car. But keep in mind that the ideal time to visit Lancaster is during the spring and fall seasons.

Intercourse—that famous mecca of shops, galleries and crafts—is closed on Sundays so if you only have a weekend to spend in Lancaster, you'll want to visit this unique village on Saturday.

The bus that takes you to Intercourse stops on Duke Street in front of the old courthouse, just a two-block walk from the Hotel Brunswick. Use your White Horse bus schedule. to check the time the bus departs. When you board the bus, ask the driver to let you off at Intercourse. Notice that there is often quite a time lag between buses but they do run on a very strict schedule, and are almost always right on time.

Intercourse brims with shops selling crafts, flowers, candles, handmade quilts and souvenirs of the Amish countryside. Most shops are owned and operated by the Amish and their horses and buggies are parked in front of banks and stores alongside tourist buses and cars. This is the town where the Amish take care of business transactions, and it's always bustling with activity.

Seated at a table next to a Mennonite couple with two perfectly behaved young children, we ate at the Intercourse Village Restaurant (in the Best Western Motel) served by young women in black pinafores and white organdy caps.

The next day, now that you've become a savvy Lancaster City bus rider, you can go to the same bus stop and use the same bus to get to Plain & Fancy Farm (note that time schedules for weekend and weekday buses are different). Ask the driver to deposit you at Plain & Fancy Farm.

Plain & Fancy consists of a nine-room farmhouse, a movie about Amish life, and a wonderful tour two-and-a-half-hour tour of the Amish countryside. The tour includes a visit to a one-room schoolhouse, a bakery and craft shop, and an Amish home.

How do you get back to the hotel when the tour is over? It's time to pull out your White Horse bus schedule. In addition to the designated bus stops, there is a flag policy and you can wave down the bus as long as you're traveling in the same direction.

If you have time after your tour is over, you can take a buggy ride or make your way over to the village of Bird-in-Hand, about a mile and a half down the road. (Most likely one of your fellow tour-takers will give you a lift. If not, it's walking distance if you're up to it—bring along your walking shoes!) Here you have time to explore the shops until your bus is scheduled to arrive at the Bird-in-Hand bus stop at Ronks Road and Old Philadelphia Pike. The bus will deposit you in front of the old courthouse.

Another alternative (for either or both trips) if you're feeling lazy or luxuriant and don't want to bus it is to call Friendly Taxi (800-795-3278) from Plain & Fancy, Bird-in-Hand, or Intercourse and have them deliver you right to the hotel door for a $28 fare. Friendly can also pick you up from the hotel and take you to any of these towns. If you are in Lancaster on a Sunday, have had your fill of "country jaunting," and want to find out about local history, you can join the one and a half-hour walking tour (sponsored by the Chamber of Commerce) that leaves at 1:30 P.M. from South Queen Street. Alternatively, you can take a swim in the indoor pool at the Brunswick and have a sumptuous brunch at Carr's. (See below.)

Eating There

We started off at House of Pizza just across Chestnut Street from the Hotel Brunswick, which features not only home-made pizza but also a full spectrum of pasta and seafood. The Lancaster Dispensing Company at Market and Orange Streets in the historic square is a lively Victorian pub that serves more than fifty varieties of beer from around the world. It offers a selection of hearty soups, sandwiches, and meat and vegetable dishes. There's a happy hour every week-day evening at 5 P.M.—"drinks for cheap"—along with complimentary hot hors d'oeuvres. Isaac's Deli at 25 North

Queen Street is a good place to grab a quick bite. At the Press Room, 26 West King Street (399-5400), you can dine on everything from burgers to full luncheons or dinners surrounded by newspaper headlines that cover the walls. Carr's Restaurant at 50 West Grant Street (299-7090) across from the Central Market serves elegant fare for lunch and dinner Tuesday through Saturday, a sumptuous Sunday brunch from 11:30-2:30, and re-opens for dinner at 4:30. Note: many restaurants are closed on Mondays . . . ask the front desk about eateries that are open on Monday.

Staying There

As mentioned throughout the chapter, we recommend staying at the Hotel Brunswick (800-233-0182) because of its ideal location. A large hotel with a comfortable lobby and clean airy rooms, the Brunswick has an indoor pool and a restaurant with a wood-burning fireplace. Every evening from 5 P.M. to 7 P.M. there is a "Happy Hour."

When you enter the lobby, pick up one of the free local newspapers to find discount coupons for restaurants and to help you locate activities such as horse and buggy rides through the countryside, sit-down dinners with an Amish family, and visits to a working Amish farm.

Index of Destinations

Atlantic City, New Jersey - 146

Baltimore, Maryland - 180

Bethlehem, Pennsylvania - 163

Boonton, New Jersey - 22

Cannondale Village, Wilton, Connecticut - - - - - - - - - - 66

Clark Gardens, New York - - - - - - - - - - - - - - - - - - - 49

Clinton, New Jersey - 72

Cold Spring, New York - 92

Dover, New Jersey - 76

Essex, Connecticut - 140

Easton, Pennsylvania - 112

Flemington, New Jersey - 78

Frenchtown, New Jersey - 81

Greenwich, Connecticut - 16

Hudson River Cruise New York Waterways, New York - - 96

Jim Thorpe, Pennsylvania - - - - - - - - - - - - - - - - - - - 170

Kingston, New York - 102

Kripalu Center, Lenox, Massachusetts - - - - - - - - - - - - 184

Kutztown, Pennsylvania - 116

Lambertville, New Jersey - 83

Lancaster, Pennsylvania - 195

Lenox, Massachusetts - 187

Long Beach, Long Island, New York - - - - - - - - - - - - - 51

Long Branch, New Jersey - - - - - - - - - - - - - - - - - - - 28

Milburn, New Jersey - 30

Milford, Pennsylvania - 118

Mitsuwa Marketplace, New Jersey - - - - - - - - - - - - - - 47

Mt. Tabor, New Jersey - 86

Mystic, Connecticut - 177

New Brunswick, New Jersey - - - - - - - - - - - - - - - - - 32

New Hope, Pennsylvania - - - - - - - - - - - - - - - - - - - 121

Nyack, New York - 106

Ocean Grove, New Jersey - - - - - - - - - - - - - - - - - - - 88

Old Bethpage Village, Long Island, New York - - - - - - - 53

Old Greenwich, Connecticut - - - - - - - - - - - - - - - - - 19

Omega Institute, Rhinebeck, New York - - - - - - - - - - - 149

Peddler's Village, Lahaska, Pennsylvania - - - - - - - - - - 125

Philadelphia, Pennsylvania - - - - - - - - - - - - - - - - - - 128

Piermont, New York - 109

Princeton, New Jersey - 37

Red Bank, New Jersey - 42

Rhinebeck, New York - 153

Rye, New York - 55

Sag Harbor, Long Island, New York - - - - - - - - - - - - - 156

Sesame Place, Pennsylvania - - - - - - - - - - - - - - - - - - 133

Silvermine Tavern, New Canaan, Connecticut - - - - - - - 68

South Norwalk, Connecticut - - - - - - - - - - - - - - - - - - 22

Southbury, Heritage Inn, Connecticut - - - - - - - - - - - - 144

Stockbridge, Massachusetts - - - - - - - - - - - - - - - - - - 191

Storm King Mountain, New York - - - - - - - - - - - - - - - 111

Tappan, New York - 58

Van Cortlandt Manor, New York - - - - - - - - - - - - - - - 62

Verona Park, New Jersey - 45

Woodstock, New York - 160

Index by State

CONNECTICUT

Cannondale Village, Wilton - - - - - - - - - - - - - - - - - - 66

Essex - 140

Greenwich - 16

Mystic - 177

Old Greenwich - 19

Silvermine Tavern, New Canaan - - - - - - - - - - - - 68

South Norwalk - 22

Southbury, Heritage Inn - - - - - - - - - - - - - - - - - 144

MASSACHUSETTS

Kripalu Center, Lenox - - - - - - - - - - - - - - - - - - - 184

Lenox - 187

Stockbridge - 191

MARYLAND

Baltimore - 180

NEW JERSEY

Atlantic City - 146

Boonton - 22

Clinton - 72

Dover - 76

Flemington - 78

Frenchtown - 81

Lambertville - 83

Long Branch - 28

Milburn - 30

Mitsuwa Marketplace - - - - - - - - - - - - - - - - - - - 47

New Brunswick - 32

Ocean Grove - 88

Princeton - 37

Red Bank - 42

Verona Park - 45

NEW YORK

Clark Gardens - 49

Cold Spring - 92

Hudson River Cruise New York Waterways - - - - - - 96

Kingston - 102

Long Beach, Long Island - - - - - - - - - - - - - - - - 51

Nyack - 106

Old Bethpage Village, Long Island - - - - - - - - - - 53

Omega Institute, Rhinebeck - - - - - - - - - - - - - - - 149

Piermont - 109

Rhinebeck - 153

Rye - 55

Sag Harbor, Long Island - - - - - - - - - - - - - - - - 156

Van Cortlandt Manor - - - - - - - - - - - - - - - - - - - 62

Woodstock - 160

PENNSYLVANIA

Bethlehem - 163

Easton - 113

Lancaster - 195

New Hope - 121

Peddler's Village, Lahaska - - - - - - - - - - - - - - - - 125

Philadelphia - 128

Sesame Place, Langhorne - - - - - - - - - - - - - - - - 133

Acknowledgments

We dedicate this book to all of the "land-locked" New Yorkers who heave a sigh at the end of summer (after their two- or four-week vacations have ended), and plunge into yet another year of unbroken daily grind in the city, dreaming and scheming about places to go for their next summer vacation, never realizing that every weekend in the year can be a heavenly "vacation" all unto its own.

We would like to thank . . .

* the innkeepers and hotel managers of lodgings described in this book, all of whom generously gave their time to introduce us to the aspects of their establishments which would best serve patrons without a car—recommending nearby eateries and providing us with the backgrounds and foregrounds of their surrounding areas, telling us where to go, what to see, and how to get there on foot or by local bus.

* The memory of Beatrice Levy, Sue's mother, who provided much enthusiastic and inspirational support for this project as she zipped around on Miami's public transportation system till she was 92 years old.

* Cynthia Nichols Mead, for recommending special destinations and accompanying us on several of our journeys.

* Jennifer Cook for her ongoing patient and generous technical assistance when the computer had tantrums and the printer went on strike.

* Jennifer Gillow for bringing up some of our prime spots online and teaching us how.to do it ourselves.

* Pace Sokolow for his constant support and for being there to listen to the tales of our travels before they were written down.

* Eric Clemett for his patience and cooperation.

* Anita Fore at the Authors Guild for her help and support through the lumps and bumps of contract interpretation.

About the Authors

Susan Clemett and Gena Vandestienne met in Greenwich Village on a park bench in Abingdon Square while their toddlers played in a sandbox. When their children became teenagers, these moms went back to school.

Susan received Masters degrees in Education and Counseling. She has been a teacher and a counselor for inner-city youth in New York public schools for many years. Gena received a Masters degree from New York University in Health and Sexuality and has been published in numerous magazines and professional journals.

Heavenly Weekends was born out of their devotion to New York City and all it provides, and their desire to venture beyond its boundaries easily and affordably—always knowing that it is there to come home to.

About the Illustrator

Molly O'Gorman is an illustrator who lives with her two children, Clara and Ted, their dog Duchess, and Trixie the cat, in Rhinebeck, New York. She is represented in the big city by Artworks Illustration.

Other City & Company Guides Available from Universe Publishing:

City Baby:
The Ultimate Guide for New York
City Parents
from Pregnancy to Preschool
2nd Edition
by Pamela Weinberg and Kelly
Ashton
$18.95
ISBN: 0-789-308-320

Literary Landmarks of New York
The Book Lover's Guide to the
Homes and Haunts
of World-Famous Writers
by Bill Morgan
$16.95
ISBN: 0-789-308-541

New York's 50 Best Places to Take
Children
2nd Edition
by Allan Ishac
$12.95
ISBN: 0-789-308-363

New York's 50 Best Places to Find
Peace & Quiet
3rd Edition
by Allan Ishac
$12.95
ISBN: 0-789-308-347

The Cool Parents' Guide to All of
New York:
Excursions and Activities In and
around Our City
That Your Children Will Love
and You Won't Think Are
Too Bad Either
by Alfred Gingold and
Helen Rogan
$14.95
ISBN: 0-789-308-592

New York's 100 Best Little Hotels
3rd Edition
by Allen Sperry
$14.95
ISBN: 0-789-308-592

And Coming Soon . . .

New York's 50 Best Places to
Enjoy Dessert
by Andrea DiNoto and Paul Stiga
$14.95
ISBN: 0-789-309-998

The New York Book of Tea
3rd Edition
by Bo Niles
$14.95
ISBN: 0-789-308-614

The New York Book of Wine
by Matthew DeBord
$14.95
ISBN: 0-789-309-971

New York's 50 Best Places to
Renew Body, Mind, and Spirit
by Beth Donnelly Cabán and
Andrea Martin, with Allan Ishac
$14.95
ISBN: 0-789-308-355